French, Cajun, Creole, Houma

FRENCH, CAJUN, CREOLE, HOUMA

A Primer on Francophone Louisiana

CARL A. BRASSEAUX

LOUISIANA STATE UNIVERSITY PRESS   *Baton Rouge*

Designer: Melanie O'Quinn Samaha
Typeface: Whitman
Printer and binder: Thomson-Shore, Inc.

Library of Congress Cataloging-in-Publication Data

Brasseaux, Carl A.
  French, Cajun, Creole, Houma : a primer on francophone Louisiana / Carl A.
Brasseaux.
      p. cm.
  Includes bibliographical references and index.
  ISBN 0-8071-3036-2 (hardcover : alk. paper)
  1. French Americans—Louisiana—History. 2. Cajuns—Louisiana—History.
3. Creoles—Louisiana—History. 4. Houma Indians—History. 5. Louisiana—
History.   I. Title.
F380.F8B735 2005
976.3'0097541—dc22

                                                              2004019011

To Betty Pellerin and Geneviève Fabre
with eternal gratitude

 Contents

 Preface

THE PRESENT VOLUME CONSISTS OF INVITED lectures, read at McNeese State University and Louisiana State University in 1999 and 2001, respectively. These essays mark the culmination of thirty years of continuous research in the area of French North America.

This lifelong interest was initially fueled by a desire to trace my own roots. Each discovery not only uncovered another piece of my family's history but also ultimately led to a better understanding of the complexity of Louisiana's cultural mosaic, a topic scholars have only begun to explore in earnest.

I sincerely hope that these essays will spark an expanded interest in Louisiana Studies by touching a new generation. Possessing life experiences and worldviews remarkably different from their predecessors, these young investigators will not only expand the envelope of knowledge but will also view the existing data from new perspectives.

FRENCH, CAJUN, CREOLE, HOUMA

CHAPTER ONE

The Remarkable Diversity of Louisiana's French-Speaking Population, 1699–1999

SINCE THE LATE 1860S WRITERS FOR THE POPular media have flocked to Louisiana in search of the state's exotic landscape, quaint settlements, and peculiar French-speaking denizens. In their quest for the unusual and the exotic, journalists have created and perpetuated stereotypes with sweeping generalizations based upon superficial impressions gathered during inevitably brief visits to the Pelican State. One of the more persistent stereotypes created by these self-proclaimed instant experts depicts Louisiana's French-speaking community as a social and cultural, sometimes even a racial, monolith. This simplistic view, which is continuously reinforced in the print and electronic media, flies in the face of recent historical, geographical, and ethnographic studies, which characterize southern Louisiana's cultural landscape as one of the most complex, if not the most complex, in rural North America.

The region's rich cultural and linguistic mosaic is the result of its role as a French melting pot, one that French ethnographer François Weil recently characterized as a unique "living laboratory." Since its establishment as a French colony in 1699, Louisiana has drawn thousands of French-speaking immigrants representing at least eighteen distinct groups, including *voyageurs*; the 1699 Canadian settlers; voluntary immigrants of the John Law era; forced immigrants of the early eighteenth century; French military personnel (many of whom opted to remain in the colony); Alsatian religious exiles;[1] Acadian exiles; Saint-Domingue refugees; refugees from the French Revolution; Bonapartist exiles; successive waves of nineteenth-century French (known within Louisiana's Francophone[2] community as *les français étrangers*), Belgian, and Swiss immigrants seeking economic opportunity; French Jews fleeing religious persecution in provinces along the German border; French, Belgian, and Canadian Catholic missionaries; Alsatian and Lorrainer refugees from the 1870 Franco-Prussian War; Lebanese Christian immigrants; twentieth-century French and

1. The scanty extant evidence suggests that, by the time of their arrival in Louisiana, the Alsatian immigrants were probably bilingual, having had to learn French to communicate with their French guards.

2. French-speaking.

Belgian war brides; European and French-Canadian teachers in the Council for the Development of French in Louisiana's bilingual programs; and Vietnamese, Cambodian, and Laotian refugees fleeing the communist takeover in their homelands. Distinctive subgroups existed within each of these immigrant groups.

Over the course of many decades following their peregrinations, many of these groups have lost their identity as they were absorbed either by more established Francophone groups in Louisiana or by America's mainstream culture. Groups undergoing the assimilation process, however, frequently retained vestiges of their parent cultures and thus remained undissolved lumps in southern Louisiana's still simmering cultural gumbo.

Louisiana's colonial heritage created the recipe by which these cultural ingredients were added, blended, and folded into the new syntheses that are now such integral parts of southern Louisiana's cultural makeup. The model for Louisiana's complex development was created with the colony's establishment in 1699. The 1699 French expedition to the Gulf Coast included at least three distinct groups of French speakers: a large party of Canadian adventurers led by future Louisiana governor Pierre Le Moyne d'Iberville, the crews manning the French naval vessels assigned to the colonization expedition, and at least fifteen buccaneers from Saint-Domingue (present-day Haiti). This simplistic grouping, of course, ignores distinctions within each group based upon class, cultural, and linguistic differences, which paled by comparison to the stark divisions separating one group from the other. Differences were especially pronounced between the Canadian and French contingents, and Louisiana's population was quickly polarized into two camps. Indeed, even when confronted by the harsh realities of frontier life which frequently threatened to overwhelm the entire colony, Canadians and Frenchmen were frequently at odds as Continental cultural and class pretensions exacerbated ethnic differences along the colony's great sociological divide.

Cultural and class antagonisms were further inflamed by the colony's demographic and economic stagnation. Louisiana was, for much of the early eighteenth century, a sparsely populated backwater outpost. Founded as a strategic outpost to neutralize the growing threat of British expansion across the North American continent, it was, as historian Mathé Allain has astutely observed, "an indispensable buffer zone between the English and the Spanish colonies." Louisiana's strategic significance, however, did not translate into rapid demographic development and unwavering royal support.

Because of the colony's military role, French Louisiana's garrison constituted the single largest component of the colonial population throughout the period of French rule (1699–1763). Only for a few fleeting years during the proprietary period (1712–31) would civilian immigration exceed the influx of soldiers. The military's dominant role in colonial life was especially pronounced in the first decades of colonization. In 1704, five years after the establishment of the French beachhead at Biloxi, the colony of Louisiana remained a military outpost including only 180 soldiers, 27 families with 10 children, and 11 Native American slaves. In 1713 there were 35 families in a colony extending from the Appalachians to the Rocky Mountains. Two years later the total population numbered only 215, 160 (74 percent) of whom were members of the French garrison.

The demographic composition of the colony began to change significantly after the colony reverted to private control. During the initial period of royal rule Pierre Le Moyne d'Iberville, Louisiana's first governor, had argued that the colony's strategic importance warranted heavy royal expenditures to underwrite the cost of transporting to the Gulf Coast large numbers of Frenchmen. Large-scale French immigration, Iberville argued, was essential if the colony was to withstand the population pressures of the neighboring British possessions, which were populated, the governor estimated, by at least 60,000 families. Iberville's petitions were neither unprecedented nor unreasonable, for the French Crown had heavily subsidized French emigration to Canada. Yet the requests of Iberville and his successors were summarily rejected by the French Crown, which, before Louis XIV's death in 1715, grudgingly agreed to provide transportation to Louisiana only to relatives of settlers already established there. The message was clear: the French monarchy was preoccupied with European affairs, particularly the nation's almost incessant warfare on the Continent, and Louis XIV's ruinously expensive capital improvements programs. Funding for the large-scale settlement of Louisiana would have to come from other sources.

Alternate sources of funding soon materialized. Unable to divert to Louisiana the meager resources necessary to maintain its small and increasingly neglected military base, Louis XIV opted to transfer control of Louisiana to French financier Antoine Crozat, with the understanding that the new colonial proprietor would send to the struggling colony annual installments of colonists. Crozat's decision to assume control of Louisiana was based primarily upon misinformation regarding the colony and its mythical mineral resources and trade opportunities provided by the French Crown and its agents. When the promised riches failed to materialize, Crozat, overwhelmed by the financial burden of administering the colony, moved quickly to cut his losses, and the anticipated influx of French settlers did not occur.

The continuing fragility of the Louisiana outpost, whose strategic importance was magnified by the French loss of Acadia in 1713, gained the attention of French authorities following Louis XIV's death. The Council of the Navy, established to administer French naval and colonial affairs during the ensuing regency of Louis XV, became concerned that, if not reinforced, the colony would either collapse or invite invasion by rival European powers.

Because of Louisiana's continuing strategic importance, the problem demanded attention, but the Crown lacked the will and the economic means to bring the matter to a satisfactory resolution. Even though the period seemed ripe for voluntary French emigration to Louisiana because inflation following the War of the Spanish Succession had reduced many poor French families to desperate circumstances, enlargement of the colony's civilian population during the regency posed a major challenge to the French government. Mathé Allain has noted that "it took exceptionally hard times to convince Frenchmen to migrate to Louisiana," but even "exceptionally hard times" could not force the nation's most destitute—and thus most eligible—families to overlook the hardships of life in Louisiana. Because these hardships were becoming increasingly well known in the coastal provinces, the government entertained no illusions about enticing the poor to emigrate voluntarily.

Even if destitute volunteers had stormed governmental offices demanding passage to Louisiana, however, there is little likelihood that they would ever have reached the colony. Nicolas Desmaretz, comptroller of royal finances, was an ardent opponent of colonial ventures because he believed that the resulting "emigration would drain France of much needed pop-

ulation." Shortly before Louis XIV's death, Desmaretz had denied Crozat's request to establish a lottery to underwrite the cost
of subsidizing French emigration to Louisiana and a subsequent
request by Jérôme Phélypeaux de Maurepas, comte de Pontchartrain, the French minister of the Navy and Colonies, to send
ten boys and ten girls to Louisiana. Desmaretz rejected the
latter request because he could not be dissuaded that twenty
emigrants "would not depopulate a kingdom of twenty million inhabitants." The Council of the Navy consequently determined to populate the colony with French criminals, vagabonds, and other "undesirables."

The French effort to bolster Louisiana's population by means
of forced emigration began in 1716, with an abortive attempt
to send to the colony a contingent of salt smugglers and girls
taken from poorhouses. Louis XIV had resisted the concept of
forced emigration on constitutional grounds, but the Sun King's
successors had no such inhibitions. Antoine Crozat, in one of
his last memos to the Crown as Louisiana's proprietor, argued
successfully that salt smugglers, who would normally have been
condemned to slavery aboard the Mediterranean galleys for having violated the royal monopoly on salt, were suitable emigrants
because the galley fleet had a surplus of oarsmen. Thus, they
would not have been missed in France. Nor did the regency
believe that the realm would miss the thousands of homeless
people who were becoming a nuisance on the streets of the

nation's capital. Disposal of such undesirables through forced emigration entailed little political risk given the considerable popular support for the deportation of nonviolent criminals because it was believed that the harsh circumstances of frontier life would force them to reform.

Having less sanguine expectations regarding the prospects of redeeming criminals and channeling them into productive lives, the Company of the West, which was chartered in August 1717 as Louisiana's new corporate proprietor, was not enthusiastic about the proposed scheme of forced emigration. Yet, because of its ties to the French stock market, the Company of the West and its successor, the Company of the Indies (1718–31), managed to generate immediate profits from its Louisiana colonization venture. Given the unlikelihood of discovering precious metals in the colony, the company's chief executive officer, John Law, understood that profits had "to come from trade, agriculture, and colonization." Law, therefore, acquiesced to political pressure from the French Crown to permit forced emigration, while, under his leadership, the company mounted an unprecedented public relations campaign to foster voluntary emigration to Louisiana.

While John Law was about the business of creating a propaganda machine, the government's plans to transport undesirables to Louisiana proceeded apace. Because of logistical problems, France's forced emigration program was slow to produce any settlers for Louisiana, and very few, if any, convicted smugglers made their way to Louisiana in 1717. By the spring of 1718 the regency had expanded the convict deportation program to include army deserters, vagabonds, beggars, prostitutes, indigents, and other outcasts. As a consequence, Louisiana became a de facto penal colony. Police dragnets established by the Regency Council in 1718 and 1719 resulted in the deportation of 1,000 to 1,200 French men and women to the Mississippi Valley. In 1721 Louisiana officials reported that forced emigrants totaled 1,278. Unsuited to frontier life, most of these deportees remained noncontributing dependents of the colonial government, establishing a criminal underworld in New Orleans.

The wholesale arrests generated a shrill outcry from the general population, prompting Louis XV to interdict all deportations to Louisiana on May 9, 1720. The negative popular image of Louisiana, however, persisted for decades afterward, resulting in a virtual halt in voluntary French emigration to the distant outpost generated by Company of the Indies propaganda.

But during its heyday the propaganda campaign had produced impressive results. The company's broadsides and propaganda tracts in the widely read *Mercure de France* contained glowing depictions of Louisiana, an idyllic land in which precious metals and gems awaited anyone with enough initiative to scratch the soil. The natives were friendly and submissive, and the soil was miraculously fertile. Despite the great expenditure of money, ingenuity, and energy in John Law's high-powered public relations campaign, disappointing numbers of voluntary emigrants materialized. Charles Le Gac, one of the company's chief agents in Louisiana, reported in his memoirs that 7,020 European immigrants reached the colony between October 25, 1717, and May 1, 1721. This figure includes 122 officers, 43 bureaucrats, 977 soldiers, 302 laborers employed by the company, 119 *concessionaires* or their agents, 2,462 indentured laborers, 1,278 salt smugglers and other forced emigrants, 1,215 women, and 502 children. Approximately 2,600 of these voluntary immigrants were German, Alsatian, and Swiss immigrants.

At first glance these numbers appear impressive, until one realizes that only 39 percent of these immigrants were expected to be immediately productive. The small overall number of laborers recruited for settlement in Louisiana despite an unprecedented advertising campaign can be attributed directly to the colony's unsavory reputation in France's Atlantic seaports. There, for example, where Louisiana had traditionally been viewed as a dangerous, Indian-infested wilderness, in which life was difficult at best, artisans were offered large monetary inducements to emigrate. Yet between 1717 and 1721 only 302 skilled workers voluntarily migrated to Louisiana. Most of these artisans were from south-central France, an area lacking direct contact with the colony. Of the 111 artisans recruited for service in Louisiana by the Company of the Indies' La Rochelle representatives in 1718 and 1719, only 8 were from the Atlantic seaports, while 89 were from the Midi.

Negative reports about Louisiana began to circulate nationally when 1,000 French and German settlers returned to France between 1719 and 1722 with stories of the deaths of hundreds of wretched voluntary and forced emigrants in Louisiana. As a consequence, popular revulsion for Louisiana had become so great in France that by 1722 voluntary emigration to the colony was stymied. Indeed, French emigration to Louisiana was reduced to such a trickle that the arrival of 95 to 120 Alsatian Lutherans condemned to religious exile in Louisiana's German Coast area in 1753 was a noteworthy demographic event.

As with French immigration, African immigration into Louisiana peaked in the early 1720s and then declined drastically. Of the 5,951 West African slaves known to have been introduced into Louisiana between 1719 and 1763, 5,470 (92 percent) arrived before 1730. Two-thirds of these slaves were drawn from Senegambia, where the Company of the Indies owned the slave concession. Louisiana documentation indicates that the vast majority of the slaves introduced during the French period were Bambara people from present-day Mali. The cultural homogeneity of these Africans facilitated the emergence of a black Creole society in the late eighteenth and early nineteenth centuries, when white planters manumitted significant numbers of their slave mistresses and natural children, thereby creating explosive growth in Louisiana's formerly small free black community. Enjoying most of the legal rights but few of the social privileges of whites, these free persons of color modeled their existences upon the lives of Louisiana's white Creole elite. They spoke French, embraced Catholicism, and, through the acquisition of slaves and extensive landholdings, established themselves as Louisiana's black elite. Their modern descendants are commonly called Creoles of Color.

Once the initial wave of African and European immigration had crashed upon Louisiana's shores in the early 1720s and then rapidly receded as death from disease, malnutrition, and exposure claimed hundreds of victims, it appeared that the colonial population would stagnate or even decline. But it did not; in 1763 there were approximately ten thousand settlers in lower Louisiana.

It is clear from all accounts that the most significant French immigration of the last four decades of the French period resulted from routine reinforcements and gradual enlargement of Louisiana's meager military garrison. Extant military, civil, judicial, and ecclesiastical records indicate that 7,104 men and women served the ancien régime in the Mississippi Valley and Gulf Coast regions; this figure does not include most of the Swiss mercenaries whose personnel dossiers have not yet been thoroughly analyzed. This impressive total belies the fact that Louisiana remained a minor outpost throughout its existence as an ancien régime colony and the fact that contemporary French officers and enlisted men considered the colony the worst posting in the empire (even worse than Cayenne, an insalubrious French possession adjacent to Devil's Island off the South American coast).

Yet many officers, enlisted men, and administrators did stay following their discharges. These royal servants–turned-settlers succumbed to the siren song of land (which was available only to the nobility in France) and economic opportunity. The number of these retirees remaining in Louisiana was restricted by royal regulations between 1731 and 1763. Extant documentation indicates that 1,421 French soldiers and Swiss mercenaries were eligible to remain in the colony as settlers. The number of soldiers who opted to remain is not known, but, if only half the eligible retirees took advantage of the opportunity, former soldiers easily constituted the largest immigrant group in post-proprietary Louisiana (1731–63). (To put this figure into perspective, the 95 to 120 Alsatian religious exiles sent to Louisiana in the 1750s form the second largest group.)

The number of soldier-settlers increased significantly following the general discharge of September 15, 1763. As a result of the 1763 Treaty of Paris, which partitioned Louisiana and transferred portions of the former French colony to Great Britain and Spain, the French monarchy ordered the dismantling of the Louisiana garrison. The colony's officers, soldiers, and administrators were given the option of remaining in Louisiana and receiving a generous land grant as well as a stipend and six months' rations to facilitate their transition to civilian life, retiring to France on a paltry pension, or continuing their service in Saint-Domingue. On May 2, 1763, Governor Louis Billouart de Kerlérec reported that half of the garrison had been placed on the roster of "old soldiers," who were evidently physically incapable of withstanding the rigors of starting life anew on the frontier. Thus, despite the great intrinsic value of the royal inducements to remain in the colony, a minority of the 1,200 to 1,300 officers, noncommissioned officers, and enlisted men in the Louisiana garrison opted to remain in the colony. Although contemporary administrative records are silent on the subject, other documentary sources suggest that approximately 280 soldiers became settlers.

Despite their sundry paths to Louisiana, these new frontiersmen came from remarkably similar backgrounds. Because there were very few volunteers, quotas for Louisiana units were often filled with captured deserters from units stationed throughout metropolitan France. Louisiana units consequently lacked the homogeneity of their metropolitan counterparts, which were usually manned by recruits from compact geographic regions. Analysis of 819 French colonial soldiers whose birthplace is known nevertheless indicates that 71 percent of these troops were drawn from just nine provinces forming a large crescent running from the Italian border through Paris to the English Channel, following the Atlantic Coast to the Bay of Biscay, moving inland in the Bordeaux region, and ending at the western border of Languedoc. Thirty-two percent of the total were drawn from two provinces: Île-de-France (the area surrounding and including Paris), which contributed 17 percent, and Brittany, which added 15 percent. The following provinces, appearing in descending order of importance, individually garnered only 4 to 6 percent of the total: Normandy, Burgundy, Poitou, Champagne, Picardy, Aunis, and Guyenne.

A sample of forty-six administrators indicates that most French colonial bureaucrats (77 percent) were drawn from the same geographical crescent that supplied most of Louisiana's military personnel. As was the case with the colonial soldiers, Île-de-France and Brittany collectively furnished disproportionately large numbers of civilian administrators (43 percent), while the provinces of Guyenne, Aunis, Champagne, and Normandy, respectively, contributed 11, 9, 7, and 7 percent of the total.

The patterns of French emigration reflected in the composition of Louisiana's military and administrative corps are also evident in the makeup of the civilian population. An analysis of the backgrounds of the 3,109 colonial era civilians whose European birthplaces are known indicates that, once again, the ancien régime provinces in the crescent are overrepresented. As in the military and administrative categories, Île-de-France and Brittany contributed one-third of the total. Aunis Province, whose major ports, La Rochelle and Rochefort, served as Louisiana's civilian and military lifelines to France, contributed an additional 10 percent, while Normandy, Champagne, Guyenne, Burgundy, and Poitou provinces each provided 4 percent of the total.

In contrast to the diversity of Louisiana's first French settlers, members of the colony's second wave of Francophone immigrants were a remarkably homogeneous group. Between 1764 and 1788 approximately 3,000 Acadian exiles made their way to Louisiana after a decade of exile and wandering throughout the northern Atlantic rim. The exiles shared unusually resilient bonds of language, kinship, and culture, all products of their historical background. Perhaps 70 percent of the original Acadian settlers were drawn in the 1630s from a single estate in northwestern Poitou Province. The Poitou emigrants, who had intermarried for generations before the onset of Acadian colonization, had easily absorbed through intermarriage the French immigrants who trickled into the colony in the late seventeenth and eighteenth centuries. By dint of intermarriage the Acadian community had become, as one observer cogently described it, a single large, highly cohesive clan. This cohesiveness permitted the community to survive the trauma of deportation and the rigors of exile.

The Acadian exiles arrived in Louisiana in five successive waves of immigration. The first consisted of twenty individuals who traveled to Louisiana from New York via Mobile, Alabama. The colonial government settled these first Louisiana Acadians along the Mississippi River near the present boundary shared by St. John and St. James parishes. Approximately 311 individuals from detention centers at Halifax, Nova Scotia, followed the 1764 immigrants. Led by the legendary Joseph Broussard *dit* Beausoleil, these Acadians arrived in New Orleans between February and May 1765; they subsequently settled in the Attakapas District, near present-day St. Martinville, before an epidemic forced them to disperse. Notified by the 1765 immigrants that Louisiana was a suitable location for the establishment of a new Acadian homeland, approximately 689 exiles in Maryland and Pennsylvania made their way to Louisiana between early 1766 and early 1770. Louisiana's new Spanish government established these refugees from the Middle Atlantic colonies in a series of settlements stretching along the Mississippi River from present-day St. James Parish to modern-day Vidalia, Louisiana.

Acadian disenchantment with the colonial government stemmed from the Spanish governor's insistence upon establishing each wave of immigrants from the Middle Atlantic colonies at different strategic sites along the Mississippi River, thereby effectively subjecting the Acadians to a second diaspora.

The resulting tensions climaxed in October 1768 with the participation of hundreds of exiles in the New Orleans uprising that drove the first Spanish governor from Louisiana. The resulting instability in the colony profoundly affected the course of the Acadian migrations, deflecting potential immigrants away from the Mississippi Valley.

The Acadian influx into Louisiana would not resume for fifteen years. In 1785, 1,596 Acadian exiles living in wretched circumstances in France's Atlantic ports boarded seven New Orleans–bound merchant vessels chartered at various French ports by the Spanish government for their transportation to Louisiana. Upon arrival at New Orleans the immigrants were housed in converted warehouses on the western riverbank. While recovering from the deleterious effects of their transatlantic voyage, they selected delegates to inspect potential home sites in lower Louisiana. On the basis of their representatives' reports, the exiles selected, on an individual basis, the most appealing settlement. Individual interests, however, were usually subordinated to those of the group, as 84 percent of the immigrants endorsed the sites recommended by their delegates. Four of the seven groups of passengers elected to establish communities along Bayou Lafourche, settling between present-day Labadieville and Raceland. Two other contingents of 1785 Acadian immigrants selected lands along the Mississippi River near Baton Rouge. The final group accepted lands along lower

Bayou des Écores (present-day Thompson's Creek). The Bayou
des Écores group was forced to relocate along Bayou Lafourche
in 1794, when a hurricane unleashed torrential rains that literally washed away their farms.

The resettlement of the Bayou des Écores Acadians marked
the final episode of the major Acadian migration to Louisiana
in the late eighteenth century. Nineteen Acadian refugees from
St. Pierre Island, a French possession off the southern Newfoundland coast, are the only exiles known to have reached
Louisiana between 1785 and 1800.

An even larger Francophone migration to Louisiana followed
hard on the heels of the end of the Acadian migration. The onset
of the French Revolution in 1789 and the black revolution in
Saint-Domingue two years later resulted in an influx of French-
speaking refugees whose scale was unprecedented in Louisiana
history. The precise number of refugees involved in this migration is difficult to determine because it is virtually impossible to distinguish the European refugees from their white
West Indian counterparts. Genealogical and historical researchers have positively identified only 14 percent of the Saint-
Domingue refugees; hence, it is not possible to distinguish
those immigrants who migrated directly from Europe from
those whose peregrinations brought them to lower Louisiana
by way of Saint-Domingue. Yet the fact that many of the French
natives had West Indian spouses suggests that dozens, perhaps

hundreds, of late-eighteenth-century French refugees had been temporary residents of the French sugar island. The relative size and demographic impact of this influx can be clearly seen by comparison of statistical profiles for French immigration before and after the start of the French Revolution: 429 French immigrants are identified in Louisiana ecclesiastical records for the period from February 10, 1763, the date of ratification for the Treaty of Paris, which partitioned French Louisiana and transferred its component parts to British and Spanish control, to December 31, 1788; 683 French natives appear for the first time in Louisiana church register entries between January 1, 1789, and December 31, 1803. The revolutionary period thus produced 63 percent more immigrants in eleven fewer years.

Our knowledge about the refugees and their wanderings is presently fragmentary, but two important generalizations nevertheless can be made about the individuals who undertook the journey to Louisiana for purposes of settlement. First, contrary to long-revered legends in New Orleans and St. Martinville, most of these French expatriates were not members of the French nobility. Indeed, only eight immigrants are clearly identified as French aristocrats in extant civil and ecclesiastical documentation for the turn of the nineteenth century, and the most notable of these nobles, the so-called Baron de Bastrop, was an imposter. This fact should hardly prove surprising, for Europeans continued to view Louisiana in much the same way that modern Americans regard the Amazon Basin. Second, many of the French refugees of the 1790s and early 1800s were drawn from French provinces that had been underrepresented in earlier historical periods. An analysis of the birthplaces for French immigrants for the period from August 19, 1769, when Governor Alejandro O'Reilly took possession of Louisiana for Spain, and December 20, 1803, when American representatives took possession of Louisiana, reveals a breakdown in the patterns of immigration which had characterized the French colonial period. Although Brittany and Île-de-France continued to contribute large numbers of immigrants, their overall importance had begun to fade, as the nation's southern provinces furnished progressively larger numbers of Louisiana settlers. The two largest contingents of immigrants were drawn from Guyenne and Provence, which respectively contributed 15 and 13 percent of the total. Brittany, Île-de-France, Normandy, Aunis, Languedoc, and Béarn round out the provinces that contributed two-thirds of Louisiana's late-eighteenth-century, non-Acadian, French immigrants.

The size of the late-eighteenth-century French influx pales by comparison to that of the Saint-Domingue refugee migration. At least 11,000 refugees from the servile insurrection in Saint-Domingue made their way to Louisiana between early 1792 and late 1809. Because of Louisiana's enduring negative reputation, only those Saint-Domingue refugees with relatives in the colony opted to sail for New Orleans during the 1790s. Gabriel DeBien and René Le Gardeur, authors of a groundbreaking study on the Saint-Domingue influx, could "identify fewer than 100 refugees who disembarked at Louisiana between 1792 and 1798." The same researchers positively identified only 26 Saint-Domingue refugees in Crescent City records for the period 1798 to 1803. In mid-1803 and "throughout 1804, [however,] hundreds of [Saint-Domingue] colonists sailing aboard ships of rather small tonnage arrived in New Orleans." Over the next five years the flow of Saint-Domingue refugees into Louisiana dwindled to a trickle, only to surge again in May 1809. Between May 1809 and January 1810, 9,059 refugees—who had been summarily expelled from their temporary homes in Oriente Province, Cuba, as a result of the Napoleonic invasion of Spain—disembarked at the Port of New Orleans. These French-speaking immigrants, who constituted Louisiana's largest and most racially diverse immigrant group to date, literally doubled the size of the Crescent City's population and preserved New Orleans' French character for two generations.

The ethnic and racial composition of the Saint-Domingue refugees of the late eighteenth and early nineteenth centuries differed significantly from their French-speaking predecessors. Between 1791 and 1809 the Saint-Domingue refugees were mostly white, although a few free persons of color and African slaves are identified in the official documentation for this influx.

The 1809 migration, however, was racially and ethnically diverse: 2,731 of the refugees were white, 3,102 were free persons of color, primarily individuals of mixed racial background, and 3,226 were black slaves.

In subsequent years the influx of West Indian refugees was limited primarily to small numbers of individuals fleeing the racial turmoil and economic instability in Martinique. The decline of Antillean immigration was offset by a European exodus, and by 1812 the focal point of Louisiana immigration had shifted once again to France.

Over the course of the nineteenth century tens of thousands of French citizens left their homeland for the New World in the wake of successive political and economic upheavals. The first nineteenth-century wave of French immigrants consisted of Bonapartists. The size of this influx is presently impossible to determine because of inadequate analysis by historians and demographers. Simone Rivière de La Souchère Deléry's once-celebrated book *Napoleon's Soldiers in America,* for example, identifies only about two dozen Bonapartist exiles who made their way to Louisiana during the first two decades of the nineteenth century, and recent findings by historian Glenn R. Conrad have made even this modest total suspect. The documentary record suggests that only a few survivors of Napoléon's failed 1803 campaign against black insurgents in Saint-Domingue made their way to the Crescent City by 1810. They were subsequently joined by the survivors of unsuccessful Bonapartist expatriate communities in Alabama and Texas. Many of these individuals were transients, and the impact of the influx on Louisiana was negligible, for the number of expatriates in Louisiana probably never exceeded two hundred.

Most of the nineteenth-century French immigrants who followed the Bonapartists were thrust upon Louisiana's shores by economic, rather than political, circumstances. Some immigrants undoubtedly left France in the wake of the country's periodic political upheavals to avoid persecution at the hands of repressive regimes. Others appear to have fled local famines or epidemics, but most appear to have had an economic incentive for relocating. The years from 1820 to 1840 constituted a transitional economic period during which Paris and France's northern provinces were rushing headlong into the nineteenth century, while the agrarian provinces unsuccessfully clung to their traditional ways of life. Many Frenchmen, particularly those with marginal job skills at the lower end of the socioeconomic spectrum, simply could not adapt to an increasingly industrialized workplace. Other residents of the industrializing provinces were the victims of periodic downturns in the local economy. Finally, many farmers were driven from the agrarian provinces by overpopulation, economic stagnation, and the decline of the linen industry, factors that collectively produced an increasingly large indigent population.

Rural and urban indigents do not appear to have played a major role in French emigration to New Orleans during the early nineteenth century, but they seem to have constituted a significant portion of all French immigrants entering the Crescent City by 1850. Federal immigration records for the port, which begin in 1820, indicate that the total number of immigrants reaching New Orleans between 1820 and 1837 was quite small, hovering between 400 and 1,500 per year. The number of French immigrants entering the Crescent City was disproportionately large during the early 1820s, constituting between 30 and 65 percent of all French immigrants to the United States. Although the percentages of the national total would decline steadily over the course of the century, New Orleans, the United States' second-leading port of entry for most of the antebellum period, continued to attract disproportionately large numbers of French immigrants until the Civil War. The passenger manifests recorded by Port of New Orleans officials indicate that 28,387 French immigrants disembarked during the period from 1820 through 1852, but only 11,552 French natives are listed in the 1850 census of Louisiana, the first decennial compilation to record nativity for every enumerated person. Many French immigrants undoubtedly fell victim to the state's notorious yellow fever and cholera epidemics or other endemic diseases, but many more were transients who migrated to the Midwest. Still others made their way to the villages dotting southern Louisiana's countryside. The most ambitious, the most talented, and the most destitute of the newcomers generally remained in New Orleans.

During the 1820s and 1830s a majority of these French immigrants—at least among those who remained in Louisiana—were merchants, artisans, and professional people. Extant New Orleans port authority records indicate that 51.38 percent of all French immigrants who disclosed their means of livelihood between 1820 and 1839 were employed in the mercantile sector. The percentage of the merchants and professionals among all French immigrants, however, declined steadily over the course of the antebellum period as the trickle of French farmers grew into a torrent. Between 1848 and 1852, for example, farmers constituted 74 percent of all French immigrants whose occupations were identified by New Orleans port authorities.

Regardless of their economic background, little is known about the birthplaces of these nineteenth-century French immigrants. Only 7 percent of the French immigrants debarking at New Orleans between 1848 and 1852, for example, indicated their place of nativity. The relatively few birthplaces that are known suggest that the so-called Foreign French were drawn from throughout the metropole, but Brittany and Alsace, both chronically impoverished and overpopulated, are heavily overrepresented among those immigrants whose birthplaces are known.

The rising tide of French immigration into Louisiana reached its zenith during the decade preceding the Civil War. The commencement of hostilities and the subsequent establishment of the Union blockade of the Gulf Coast in 1861 disrupted the influx, while widespread wartime destruction and the virtual collapse of the state's rural economy in the early Reconstruction period collectively diverted French emigrants to New York and other northern ports. The once impressive flow of French immigrants into New Orleans was reduced to a trickle, as can be seen in the steadily declining numbers of French immigrants reportedly residing in Louisiana in each of the decennial federal census reports between 1860 and 1920 (see table 1).

The movement of other French-speaking groups into Louisiana during the post–Civil War period could not offset the precipitous decline in French immigration. The most notable of these immigrant groups were Francophone Belgians, Swiss, and Lebanese Christians, yet they numbered only 350, 378, and 954, respectively, in the 1920 federal census of Louisiana.

The declining numbers of French-speaking immigrants persisted after the conclusion of the two world wars, despite the arrival of numerous French war brides after 1945. By 1970 the number of French natives residing in Louisiana had fallen to 1,002, the lowest total since the 1710s. The establishment of the Council for the Development of French in Louisiana's bilingual

TABLE 1. FRENCH NATIVES LIVING IN LOUISIANA, 1850–1990

YEAR	NUMBER
1850	11,552
1860	14,938
1870	12,341
1880	9,992
1890	8,437
1900	6,500
1910	5,302
1920	4,182
1930	2,935
1940	1,840
1950	1,521
1960	1,357
1970	1,002
1980	1,491
1990	1,350

educational program in the early 1970s—a program that, at its peak, annually brought to Louisiana 300 French instructors—temporarily halted the persistent decline in French immigration into Louisiana. The number of resident French aliens increased to 1,491 in 1980, but the downward spiral soon resumed, in part because of Louisiana's falling economic fortunes, and, by 1990 the total had dwindled to 1,350. Most of the latter-day French immigrants were urbanites residing in southern Louisiana municipalities; indeed, 49 percent of the transplanted French natives resided in either the Greater New Orleans or Baton Rouge areas.

The brief upturn in French immigration coincided with the movement of other French speakers into the Pelican State. The latter migration consisted of refugees from former French Indochina, particularly Vietnamese and Laotians, for whom French was a second language. There were 728 Vietnamese natives in Louisiana in 1980; 79 of these individuals moved to Louisiana between 1970 and 1974, while an additional 634 immigrants migrated to the state between 1975 and 1980. They were accompanied by Laotian immigrants, who numbered 1,018 in the 1990 census of Louisiana. Most of the Vietnamese refugees settled in the Versailles subdivision of eastern New Orleans, but hundreds of others migrated to the state's coastal parishes, where they resumed their lives as fishermen. The Laotians, on the other hand, have congregated in Iberia Parish, where they have established insular agrarian communities.

The conventional wisdom has been that these refugees from former French Indochina congregated in Louisiana because of the region's climate, vibrant fishing industry, Catholic heritage, and enduring French language. Scholarly investigations into the Asian refugee communities, however, make it abundantly clear that language was not a significant consideration, for "less than 10 percent" of the immigrants—primarily members of the elite who had been educated in French colonial schools—actually spoke French fluently.

As the Laotian and Vietnamese experiences make abundantly clear, the role of twentieth-century immigration—with the notable exception of the CODOFIL teachers—in sustaining Louisiana's French language and culture was virtually nil. Like their Francophone predecessors of the eighteenth and nineteenth centuries, the various French-speaking groups who have migrated to Louisiana since 1900 selected divergent courses of adaptation to their adopted homeland. Yet for all these disparate groups the paths led to the same destination—mainstream American society. Like their counterparts elsewhere in the United States, the various Francophone immigrant groups of the nineteenth and twentieth centuries followed the classical three-generational model of assimilation as set out by the United States Bureau of the Census—monolingual non-English-speaking immigrants; bilingual first-generation Americans of "foreign stock"; and monolingual English-speaking, second-generation Americans who were full participants in America's dominant culture.

The steady march of Louisiana's French immigrants into the American mainstream was accelerated by the sharp decline in French immigration following the onset of the Civil War. No longer sustained by a steady flow of economic and political refugees, the Pelican State's Foreign French community was unable to maintain its cultural base. The community's rapid disintegration is seen most clearly in the disappearance in the late nineteenth century of the bilingual rural newspapers whose French sections were targeted at the Foreign French. Even in New Orleans, once the nation's second-leading port of entry for Francophone immigrants, the Foreign French readership had dwindled to such an extent that the city's last French-language newspaper, *L'Abeille de la Nouvelle Orléans,* was compelled to cease publication on December 27, 1923, after more than ninety-six years of service. Although French immigrants organized their own benevolent societies and annually celebrated Bastille Day, their descendants made no effort to preserve their linguistic and cultural heritage. This had profound ramifications for the course of French Louisiana's development because it meant that European immigrants played a highly circumscribed role in the evolution of the three major ethnic and linguistic communities that had taken root in lower Louisiana during the colonial era.

The heirs of these three colonial cultural traditions are, of course, white Creoles, Creoles of Color, and Cajuns. The oldest of the white Francophone communities, established by French and Canadian immigrants of the early eighteenth century, created a new cultural synthesis in the Mississippi Valley frontier. A new cultural synthesis was necessary because of the diverse backgrounds of the colony's French immigrants, who, despite their shared difficulties, had little in common with one another besides their feudalistic background. Prior to the twentieth century France was a patchwork of highly distinctive subregions whose linguistic, cultural, legal, and social traditions were often incompatible. Parisians, for example, did not speak the same language as natives of Languedoc or Provence, and Bretons typically could not communicate with these groups. Nor could the French Basques, German-speaking Alsatians and Lorrainers, and Italian-speaking natives of the Piedmont area along the Franco-Italian border—an area now part of France. In the isolation of Louisiana, however, French frontiersmen needed effective communication skills to survive; hence, the language of the French capital, which also constituted the linguistic standard for official communications within the colony, became the lingua franca, and, although it has since come to be known as "colonial French" in Louisiana, it is, in fact, standard French, the language that originated in the Île-de-France region.

African slaves introduced into French Louisiana faced the same linguistic dilemma. Although a plurality of the Africans deposited on Louisiana's shores in the 1720s were members of the Bambara tribe of present-day Mali, slaves imported into Louisiana in the late eighteenth century were drawn from an enormous geographical region of sub-Saharan Africa. Because linguistic diversity within the slave community was infinitely more complex that in its white counterpart, Africans, like the French immigrants themselves, soon came to utilize French (and to a lesser extent the hybrid language Creole) as the basis for interpersonal communications. Unlike their French-speaking neighbors, the Acadians, products of an earlier colonial melting pot, spoke a seventeenth-century patois from the Centre-Ouest region of France; although distinctive, the dialect was sufficiently compatible to permit effective communications between the Acadians and their Francophone neighbors, both black and white.

Linguistic diversity within Louisiana's white Francophone communities was underscored by disparate, conflicting worldviews that continuously underscored the social and cultural differences dividing the three groups. The most pronounced differences divided the Acadian and white Creole communities. Louisiana's French immigrants of the early eighteenth century sought to re-create along the Mississippi's banks the feudalistic society they had left behind—making themselves the aristocracy. The hierarchical society that they created was given impetus by the force of tradition and the black code of 1724, which created a three-tiered racial hierarchy, consisting, in descending order, of whites, free persons of color, and slaves. Such a hierarchical system was anathema to the Acadians, who had sprung from peasant stock and who had spent 150 years casting off the shackles of feudalism, and they bitterly resented the efforts of white Creoles to cast them in the role of a colonial peasantry. In the resulting culture clash white Creoles and Acadians came to occupy the polar extremes of the hierarchy in the white community. Upwardly mobile Acadians found themselves in a socioeconomic niche dominated by white Creoles, while downwardly mobile Creoles (and other whites) came to be identified with the lowly Acadians. Because there was much more downward mobility among rural Louisianians over the course of the eighteenth and nineteenth centuries, Acadian/ Cajun society became the locus of the region's most notable melting pot. Cajun music and Cajun cuisine are both twentieth-century products of this melting pot, and the process continues, as the following quotation clearly indicates. In February 1999 Johnny Nguyen, a 1975 immigrant from Saigon now residing in Vermilion Parish, informed Lafayette reporter Bernard Chaillot: "You know, a lot of us [Vietnamese] are honorary Cajuns now, too. We love to play bourée." With such ingredients in the pot, there will undoubtedly be new flavors of French Louisiana's cultural gumbo in the twenty-first century.

CHAPTER TWO

Four Hundred Years of Acadian Life in North America

It had a half chapter about our state's [Indiana's] political climate, as so far as I could tell, it must have been written after a careful examination of the situation in California.

Arnold Sawislak

THE DISTORTED VIEW FROM THE OUTSIDE

THE ACADIANS ARE PERHAPS AMERICA'S MOST enigmatic people, equally misunderstood by outsiders and members of the group itself. This shroud of misunderstanding is the legacy of the group's unique North American experience, the co-optation of its leadership element by the regional socioeconomic elites, and the creation and persistence of conflicting (uncomplimentary and complimentary) stereotypes by generations of popular American writers, journalists, and filmmakers. These arbiters of America's popular perceptions have generally visited the bayou country too briefly to acquire accurate impressions of the area and its inhabitants, and their depictions of Cajuns constantly reinforce the existing popular misconceptions about Acadiana.

The quantity of misinformation distributed by Hollywood and the popular press is, naturally, inversely proportional to the writers' degree of familiarity with their subjects, and, unfortunately for Louisiana's Acadians, these conceptual problems are compounded by the condescension and rancor of many American writers. Apparently because of the absence of an Acadian Defense League, critics have been completely uninhibited in casting aspersions against southern Louisiana French speakers, promulgating throughout the nation epithets that they would not dare to use in private conversations when referring to other American racial and cultural minorities. Thus, for most North Americans, and many Europeans, Louisiana remains a lost paradise—an exotic land, populated by even more peculiar French-speaking primitives, the Acadians. In this illusory image of Acadiana, Acadians, descendants of Louisiana's eighteenth-century Acadian immigrants, are inevitably poor, inbred, ignorant, hedonistic, unambitious, and sinister swamp dwellers leading an idyllic, if not indolent, existence against the backdrop of North America's most backward, corrupt, and exploitative political and economic systems.

Far less numerous than the detractors of Acadians/Cajuns are the group's apologists. Cajun apologists have traditionally viewed Acadians as the twentieth century's version of the Jeffersonian yeoman—honest but backward trappers, farmers, and fishermen who have rejected the evils of modern materialism for the simple rewards of rural living. The perceived ability of Acadian swamp and marsh dwellers to live harmoniously with their environment has drawn particular praise.

These conflicting but equally flawed perceptions of the Acadians betray the limited vision of their creators. In their quest for the unusual and the exotic, journalists have traditionally failed to perceive the complexity of modern Acadian society. Indeed, these writers have generally failed to comprehend that Acadians constitute a complete, highly stratified, and now heavily urbanized society, living in highly diverse economic and topographic environments. A "typical" Acadian might now be a banker, truck driver, architect, mechanic, physician, farmer, public school teacher, trapper, realtor, shrimper, oilfield worker, engineer, welder, university professor, police officer, plumber, electrician, or lawyer, living in an equally broad range of house types and topographic subregions.

The Underlying Truth

Had early investigators of the Acadian experience bothered to scrutinize carefully the documentation left behind by the Acadian people, their characterization of the Acadian experience would have been entirely different. Viewed from the perspective of the documentary record, as well as the oral traditions that have survived within the community itself, it is clear that the story of the Acadians is one of survival against all odds. Indeed, the Acadians have been very much like the coastal marshes, one of the most distinctive topographic features of their native French provinces, their pre-dispersal Canadian settlements, and their adopted Louisiana homeland. Although continuously buffeted by winds and tides and thus continuously changing, these fragile ecosystems somehow find the means to endure. Even when overwhelmed by periodic flooding, they simply absorb the resulting sediment, adapt to the new environment, and regenerate with greater resilience and vigor.

FRENCH ORIGINS AND EARLY COLONIAL EXPERIENCES

The origins of the Acadian saga can be traced to the late sixteenth and early seventeenth centuries—a time not so different from our own. Because of modern America's preoccupation with race, it is easy to forget that religion and class have constituted humanity's most profound and enduring agents of social division. From the mid-sixteenth century until 1628, France was ravaged by religious warfare between the nation's Catholic majority and Huguenot minority. Protestantism was introduced into France between 1520 and 1523, and the Huguenots,

French Calvinist Protestants, claimed many adherents among the French nobility, intellectual classes, and mercantile classes. Protestantism enjoyed phenomenal growth in France in the late 1550s and early 1560s, and the inroads made in this traditional bastion of Roman Catholicism generated considerable concern among the country's ecclesiastical and secular authorities. The resulting repression elicited a violent response, producing a series of eight civil wars between 1562 and 1598.

France's religious warfare resulted in the establishment of Acadia. During the brief respites between the fighting, Huguenot merchants, who controlled much of France's maritime fleet, utilized their resources in attempts to establish a religious haven in the New World. Huguenots first attempted to plant a colony in the Americas in present-day Brazil in 1555. This outpost was destroyed by Portuguese forces in March 1560, after intense fighting. French Protestants attempted to establish a second beachhead in Florida in 1562 and again in 1564. Like its predecessor, the settlement was destroyed by military force, this time mobilized by Spanish authorities at St. Augustine, Florida. Driven out of the subtropical zones of North and South America by force of arms, the Huguenots made a final attempt to lay the foundation for a New World colony on the "brutally inhospitable northern coast," where French explorers and, later, fishermen had established a tenuous claim to the territory.

French colonization along the Bay of Fundy grew out of an

attempt by Huguenot Pierre du Guay, sieur de Monts, to exploit the fur trade in eastern Canada. In 1603 de Monts acquired a ten-year monopoly over the region's fur trade and fisheries. After a nearly disastrous winter at Île St. Croix (present-day Dorchet Island, Maine), during which 35 of the 125 French settlers died of scurvy, de Monts transferred the colony to Port Royal, in present-day Nova Scotia. There the colonists erected a trading post and established amicable relations with the neighboring Micmac Indians. As a result of a growing Native American desire for French trade goods, the Port Royal trading post quickly proved successful. De Monts returned to France in 1605 with a small cargo of pelts. Yet, upon his arrival in the mother country, the colonial proprietor discovered that his monopoly had been revoked, necessitating the evacuation of Port Royal in 1607.

In 1610, however, Port Royal was reoccupied by Jean de Biencourt de Poutrincourt, who had acted as governor of Acadia during the ill-fated de Monts proprietorship. Although the colony consisted of only twenty-five men, Poutrincourt and his son and successor, Charles de Biencourt de St. Just, laid the foundation for a permanent settlement. Upon the return of French colonists to Port Royal, the fur trade was reestablished, and crops were sown, yet the French presence in the colony remained tenuous at best. Religious warfare in France prevented the proprietors from reinforcing the settlement, making it easy prey for foreign invaders. In 1613 English privateer Samuel Argall attacked and destroyed Port Royal. The colony never fully recovered from Argall's raid, and, after Biencourt's death in 1623, the small band of French adventurers remaining in the Bay of Fundy Basin became so demoralized that they were unable to prevent the colonization of Scottish Calvinists at Port Royal in 1628–29. Yet the French colony somehow survived despite the defeat of the last Protestant bastion at La Rochelle by Catholic forces in 1628, establishing a precedent in the Acadian community which has endured to the present.

Driven from Port Royal and virtually abandoned by France as religious warfare escalated in the metropole, Acadia's French colonists continued their fur-trading operations from Cape Sable under the leadership of Charles de St. Etienne de La Tour. These activities maintained France's claim to the region until it reverted to official French control in 1632 through the Treaty of St. Germain-en-Laye.

After 1632 France's Catholic monarchy, acting through the Company of New France, began to encourage New World colonization. In 1632 three hundred French settlers, commanded by newly appointed Governor Isaac de Razilly, organized themselves into paramilitary units at the mouth of La Hève River, reoccupied Port Royal in early September and expelled all but a handful of the Scottish colonists there.

Although the reinforcement of the tiny French colony in Acadia seemed to augur the beginning of a golden era of colonization in the Bay of Fundy, that promise was never realized because of the French government's intervention in colonial affairs. In a classic example of the late ancien régime policy of placing colonial leaders in competitive (if not confrontational) situations, Cardinal Richelieu, French minister of state and architect of French absolutism, awarded La Tour and Razilly large estates and exclusive fur-trading zones with overlapping boundaries. The resulting tensions erupted into civil warfare following Razilly's death in 1635. Rival fur trappers frequently engaged in "skirmishes, blockades, fort-storming, and the capture and recapture of [trading] posts." Fighting ceased only in 1650.

The resulting tranquillity within the colony was short-lived. In 1654 the British seized Acadia, and the colony remained in British hands for sixteen years.

The British occupation of Acadia brought to a close the turbulent half-century in which Acadian society assumed its national character. The survival of the French community was a direct consequence of the population's makeup. Between 1632 and 1654, when most of its French colonists crossed the Atlantic for the Bay of Fundy Basin, Acadia was a proprietary colony operated by the Company of New France. The company maintained a recruiting office operated by Vincent Landry in La

Chaussée, Poitou Province, France. At least 55 percent, and possibly as much as 70 percent, of Acadia's seventeenth-century immigrants were natives of either the Centre-Ouest provinces of Poitou, Aunis, Angoumois, and Saintonge or Anjou Province, in an adjacent geographical region. All of these ancien régime provinces were located southeast and east-southeast of Brittany. Forty-seven percent were drawn from the La Chaussée area alone. At least twenty-two of the fifty-two families listed in the 1671 census of Acadia—42.3 percent of the total—were drawn from the estate of Charles Menou d'Aulnay, acting governor of Acadia for much of the proprietary period. The Aulnay estate lay approximately three and a half miles northwest of the La Chaussée recruiting office. In 1644 alone, Aulnay, who had personally undertaken a disastrous recruiting tour of the Centre-Ouest four years earlier, hand-picked at least twenty peasant families (approximately sixty persons) on his estate for settlement as Acadia colonists. Many other recruits—perhaps six additional families—were also evidently drawn from the Aulnay estate or from the city of Loudun, the regional commercial and religious center located 10.62 linear miles north of La Chaussée. (These recruits, and those who followed, were compelled by the monarchy to become at least nominally Catholic.)

These immigrants constituted the nucleus of Acadia's early colonial population. Their demographic dominance persisted despite the trickle of French immigrants into Acadia between

1671 and 1713 because of the core group's remarkable fecundity. In 1671 families of the La Chaussée area constituted between 40 and 54 percent of the total Acadian population, depending upon whether or not those probably recruited in the Aulnay estate / Loudun area are included in the total. By the twentieth century this core group's descendants had come to constitute between 80 and 90 percent of the total Acadian population in the Canadian Maritimes and a corresponding proportion of Louisiana's Acadian community.

Acadia's French pioneers also shared a common socioeconomic background. According to the 1671 census of Acadia, forty-eight of the sixty-three male heads of households (76 percent) were *laboureurs*. This designation was utilized in ancien régime France to designate the nation's most prosperous peasants, who constituted "a kind of peasant-aristocracy [that] owned enough land to make a good living from it." *Laboureurs* often tilled five or more hectares (at least 11.15 acres), for which they had to provide the necessary farming implements, carts, and teams of work animals. To succeed they had to coax from exhausted soils crop yields sufficiently large both to sustain their own farming operation and to pay the heavy fees levied by the nobility for use of the lands.

Laboureurs, who were noted for their industriousness, were a vital cog in late ancien régime agriculture, and they constituted the keystone of Acadia's economic development. But why did they abandon their seemingly secure and prosperous homes for the rigors of colonial life? Their departure for the New World is all the more intriguing because the French farming classes of this period were characterized as "très sédentaire parce que physiquement attaché au sol natal."[1]

The evidence suggests that they sought to escape the violence that had disrupted their lives and destroyed in a matter of years the modest wealth accumulated over generations. Because Poitou Province and the Centre-Ouest region were bastions of sixteenth- and seventeenth-century French Protestantism, these areas were the scenes of some of the most intense combat during France's religious wars. Fighting between Catholic and Protestant communities erupted at Poitiers in 1559, and within two years the entire region was consumed by the increasingly vicious civil warfare. Much of the fighting in the 1560s centered in the upper Poitou Province area, from which most of the original Acadian settlers were drawn. The Aulnays, then solidly in the Huguenot camp, were among three upper Poitou families who organized a major military offensive that succeeded in capturing Loudun and several other major Poitevin cities.

The Protestant occupation of these communities was challenged by Catholic forces, and the resulting confrontations,

1. "Very sedentary because physically attached to native soil."

which continued until the Edict of Nantes of 1598 established a national policy of religious tolerance, ravaged the entire region. Indeed, many of the worst atrocities of the French religious wars were committed in Poitou during the intense internecine fighting, and the local civilian population had to be constantly on guard against marauding bands of religious fanatics, foraging mercenaries, and brigands capitalizing upon the breakdown of local law enforcement. The civilians were nevertheless frequently subjected to "pillages, fires, thefts, tortures, and massacres." These assaults upon the peasantry continued throughout the religious wars.

The end of the religious wars in 1628 brought precious little relief to the upper Poitou area. Years of unseasonable weather brought famine and a series of epidemics, the plague of 1631 being the worst epidemic in modern French history. The plague decimated the population between Poitiers and the Atlantic Ocean. Pestilence was accompanied by famine. The emotional stresses occasioned by years of civil strife, the general breakdown in law and order, epidemics, the threat of starvation, and, finally, the famous Loudun witch-hunt of 1634 evidently proved more than many La Chaussée *laboureurs* were willing to tolerate. For these new pioneers the hardships of the frontier were more palatable than the misery they had left behind.

During their first years in the New World the former peasants had ample cause to reconsider their decision. The new colonists had fled one civil war in their homeland only to find themselves in the midst of another internecine conflict in Acadia. The resulting hardships were compounded by the fact that the colony was largely neglected by France. As a consequence, Acadia fell prey to frequent incursions by France's military rivals. Indeed, the colony changed hands ten times between 1604 and 1713.

The absence of stability in seventeenth-century Acadia forced the colonists to adapt to harsh new surroundings with virtually no outside assistance. The Acadian colonists found strength in their remarkably cohesive families to overcome new challenges, and, when precedents for such adaptation existed, particularly when dealing with local authority figures, the colonists fell back upon their experiences as peasants. As French peasants, the colonists had had to rely upon their wits to survive. Unable to achieve what was then unthinkable—a fundamental change in the system—the peasants attempted, often successfully, to shield themselves from their overlords through trickery, by feigning ignorance, or, more commonly, by resorting to "passive disobedience." Passive disobedience usually took the form of procrastination in completing contracted tasks, delayed payments of use fees, or fictitious crop shortages to avoid, or at least reduce, levies on their harvests. Such resistance was successful only when the peasantry joined ranks and presented a united front against landlords. Peasants in the

Poitou and Centre-Ouest, which had France's most intricate and cohesive extended family system, had long experience in utilizing these techniques effectively, and the transplanted *laboureurs* used them quite successfully against French and, later, British colonial authorities. The colonists, for example, routinely failed to meet their crop quotas under the pretext of unseasonable weather while surreptitiously exporting significant crop surpluses.

The resulting spirit of independence was reinforced by frequent changes in domination of the colony, by the colony's geographic isolation, and by the mother country's neglect of Acadia. These circumstances produced three immediate results. First, the Acadians became the first group of European colonists to develop a distinctive North American identity. Second, the Acadians were forced to think and act for themselves; as in feudalistic France, the former peasants elected delegates to represent their interests in negotiations with authority figures. Third, the Acadian colonists quickly came to realize that, as in sixteenth- and seventeenth-century France, identification with belligerents held the promise of immediate and dire consequences. The local Micmac Indians, whose numbers in the early eighteenth century matched those of the Acadians, were staunch allies of the French, and the colonists feared reprisals if they aligned themselves with France or Great Britain in their ongoing struggle for regional hegemony. The Acadian community consequently chose the path of official neutrality (while simultaneously providing some surreptitious assistance to the Micmac), which, of all possible options, held the best possibility of deliverance from the almost incessant warfare that had plagued their world.

BIRTH OF AN IDENTITY

The group's independent spirit, cohesiveness through extensive familial networking that eventually transformed the population into one large clan, and the Acadians' notorious stubbornness made it virtually impossible for the administrators to impose their will upon the group. This is seen most clearly in the initial British attempts to extract an unconditional oath of allegiance from the colonists. The British, who acquired the colony, which they dubbed Nova Scotia, through the Treaty of Utrecht in 1713, were always greatly outnumbered by their reluctant Acadian subjects. British colonial officials were thus extremely anxious to bring the Acadians into their camp through an iron-clad oath of allegiance. Negotiations to procure the oath, which began with the British conquest of Acadia in 1710, were concluded only in 1730. For twenty years Acadian delegates refused to accept an oath without guarantees of Acadian neutrality in the event of future Anglo-French conflicts. In 1730 the Acadian representatives acquiesced only after receiving unauthorized, and quite spurious, verbal assurances from the British colonial governor that the Acadians would enjoy neutral status in future confrontations between the French and British empires.

LE GRAND DÉRANGEMENT

Over the next two decades the Acadians generally honored their commitment to neutrality during intercolonial warfare, despite French-Canadian attempts to incite Bay of Fundy area settlers to revolt. British officials nevertheless remained uneasy about their Acadian subjects, particularly after 1750, when a French Catholic missionary ordered his Micmac parishioners to burn a large Acadian village in order to force its inhabitants into French-held territory and ultimately into the local French militia. The British colonial government responded to this external threat by attempting to extract, once again, an unconditional oath of allegiance from Nova Scotia's now large and rapidly growing population (see table 2). Still unwilling to be caught in yet another crossfire, the Acadians refused British demands and insisted that they would in no way alter the terms of the 1730 conventions.

By unswerving adherence to the "conventions of 1730," the Acadians in 1750 had foiled a British attempt to undermine their semiautonomous position in the colony. Unqualified subservience to the British colonial regime, many contemporary British observers and many historians of the Acadian diaspora

TABLE 2. ACADIAN POPULATION GROWTH, 1654–1755

YEAR	POPULATION
1654	300–350
1701	1,450
1737	7,598
1755	12,000–18,000

agree, was the first step in an evolving British plan for assimilating the potentially subversive, French-speaking Catholics into the Anglo-Protestant mainstream of the British Empire. Failing that, British authorities wished to confiscate for proper British Protestants the Acadian settlements, which contained the best farmland along the northern Atlantic coastline.

This eventuality was not lost upon the Acadian leaders. Although their struggle against the British colonial regime was couched in political terms, the Acadians were actually fighting for their ethnic survival. The Acadians were given a brief reprieve during the gubernatorial administration of the conciliatory Peregrine Hopson, but the growing border tensions between the French and British North American empires embroiled the reluctant British subjects once again in a power struggle with the colonial government, recently installed at Halifax.

Suspicious of Acadian motives and no longer dependent upon the good graces of the French-speaking community for its survival, the ruling English oligarchy now resolved to settle the festering Acadian problem once and for all. The fate of the Acadian population lay with the Nova Scotian governor and colonial council, in whose hands all authority was vested by the colonial charter. The chief executive, however, played a pivotal role in shaping the British response to the recently resurrected Acadian problem.

In 1754 Major Charles Lawrence succeeded Hopson as governor of Nova Scotia. A professional soldier who had most recently served on Nova Scotia's western border strengthening the colony's defenses against the growing French military threat, Lawrence was preoccupied with the vulnerability of the colony he now commanded. And, in Lawrence's mind, the internal threat posed by the Acadians had to be crushed in a manner disturbingly reminiscent of another "final solution."

Despite Lawrence's increasingly shrill calls for Acadian capitulation to his demands for unconditional fealty to the British monarch, the French-speaking colonists saw no reason to alter their traditional demand for neutrality. And, as their population, which now numbered between twelve and eighteen thousand persons, easily dwarfed its English counterpart, the Acadians did not feel intimidated by British threats. Failing to perceive the growing paranoia of Lawrence and other key figures in the colonial government, the Acadians exhibited no interest whatsoever in linking their collective destiny with that of the British Empire. In 1750 the Acadians had witnessed with horror the fiery destruction of the heavily populated Beaubassin district by French-allied Micmacs, and the increasing belligerence of the French forces along Nova Scotia's borders augured ill for anyone in the British camp.

The refusal of the Acadians to comply with Lawrence's demands for a new, unconditional oath of allegiance prompted Nova Scotia's acting governor to put into motion his scheme to remove the Acadian population from its homeland. In late spring 1755 eighteen hundred British soldiers from New England sailed to the Isthmus of Chignecto, connecting Nova Scotia to the Canadian mainland. The troops seized the French installations along the border, then Lawrence demanded that the Acadians surrender their firearms. Deprived of their weapons and barred from escape, the Acadians were completely at the mercy of the British.

Lawrence was quick to exploit this advantage. In late June 1755 he ordered all Acadian settlements in Nova Scotia to send delegates to the colonial capital ostensibly to discuss the possible return of confiscated Acadian firearms. When the delegation representing the Mines area—the most thickly populated Acadian settlements in the Bay of Fundy Basin—appeared before the governor on July 3, however, Lawrence demanded that they accept, on behalf of their constituents, an unconditional oath of allegiance to Britain. The Acadian delegates stubbornly refused to concede their neutral status, and they consequently were summarily imprisoned to serve as an example to their equally recalcitrant constituents.

The refusal of the Mines delegation to accede to Lawrence's demand created a crisis of authority in the colony, one exacerbated by the arrival on July 23 of reports of General Edward Braddock's humiliating defeat by a small French and Indian force in the Middle Atlantic colonies. This news, and the impending hostilities that it foreshadowed, made the colonial council all the more inclined to support Lawrence's intractable position regarding the Acadians. On July 31, 1755, that body ordered the wholesale deportation of the Acadian population.

To effect the removal as expeditiously and as cheaply as possible, Lawrence devised a scheme for ensuring the Acadians' peaceable submission to deportation. Drawing upon engineer Charles Morris's memorandum on Acadian deportation, Charles Lawrence directed the English commandants at Beaubassin, Pisiquid, and Annapolis-Royal to lure local Acadian males into their respective posts. There the unsuspecting victims would be arrested and detained until the arrival of transports that would carry them into exile. The detention of male hostages would ensure that the local women and children would remain home with their possessions and livestock, thus expediting their removal from the colony. Finally, all Acadian property would be confiscated to reimburse the Nova Scotian government for the cost of the Acadians' removal. All Acadian homes and boats were to be destroyed to discourage the deportees from returning.

This plan was implemented with ruthless precision by the British commandants in the Beaubassin and Pisiquid / Grand Pré areas. Implementation was far less effective at Annapolis-Royal (formerly Port Royal), where the local Acadians, fearing a trap, fled into the woods. Only the onset of winter forced the Acadians there to capitulate.

The Acadian deportees removed from Annapolis-Royal, Pisiquid / Grand Pré, and Beaubassin numbered approximately fifty-four hundred individuals. Deportations continued on a smaller scale in subsequent years. Historians estimate that approximately six thousand Acadians had been sent into exile by 1760.

The exiles were dispersed among the English seaboard colonies from Georgia to Massachusetts. Those who were deemed most dangerous to British interests because they had served as French conscripts were sent to Georgia, the colony farthest from Nova Scotia. Virginia refused to receive its contingent of exiles, who contracted smallpox during the voyage, and these unfortunate detainees were sent to England. At least half their number perished during the voyage.

The unspeakable sufferings of the exiles sent to Britain was shared by those Acadians in the seaboard colonies. During the

passage the exiles endured conditions similar to those of the
Middle Passage. Crammed into dank, dark holds of their small
British transport vessels, given substandard food and water, and
denied knowledge of their destination, the Acadian deportees
were a miserable lot indeed. As the Acadians exiled to Pennsylvania subsequently recalled: "we were so crowded on the
transport vessels, that we had not room even for all our bod-
ies to lay down at once, and consequently were prevented from
carrying with us proper necessities." Extant documentation
reveals that the typical British transport carried one-third more
passengers than it was designed to hold. The result of the over-
crowding, poor diet, and contact with sailors who were carriers
of the twin scourges of the eighteenth century—smallpox and
typhus—was a staggering death toll, a toll in human lives that
continued after exiles reached their destinations. During the
period of wanderings which began in 1763 and continued until
the mid-1780s, this scenario was repeated as the exiles succumbed to malnutrition, exposure, and disease. Scholars now
estimate that at least half of the Acadian population perished
during the Grand Dérangement, and fifty years would elapse
before Acadian population figures reached their pre-dispersal
levels.

Despite the physical and emotional trauma endured by the
exiles during the dispersal and the subsequent period of wanderings, the Acadians' spirit remained unbroken. The Acadians

exiled to Georgia secured ten small sailing vessels and then embarked upon an attempt to return home. These peripatetic refugees were arrested and placed in detention centers when they reached New York. Large numbers of Acadians exiled to South Carolina attempted to escape into the North American interior.

The Acadians detained in the Middle Atlantic colonies enjoyed much less mobility. They were treated as de facto prisoners of war, but, as British subjects by virtue of the Conventions of 1730, they were accorded none of the rights of prisoners of war. In January 1757, for example, the Pennsylvania legislature passed a bill requiring all Acadian exiles in the colony to apprentice their children to English-speaking artisans as a means of both removing them from the government dole and compelling them to assimilate. The Pennsylvania Acadians loudly protested this heavy-handed effort to destroy their families. Asking whether they were "subjects, prisoners, slaves, or freemen," the Acadians in Philadelphia demanded permission to leave the colony. The Pennsylvania government officially disregarded the Acadian protest, but it did not enforce the apprenticeship legislation. When the government ignored them, the Pennsylvania Acadians publicly announced their intention of joining French forces in Canada or Louisiana and fighting the Anglo-Pennsylvanians. Their "mutinous" spirit was sufficiently threatening to attract the attention of Lord

Loudoun, commander-in-chief of British forces in North America, who ordered the arrest of several prominent Pennsylvania Acadians in an attempt to end such insubordination. The Acadians responded with a remonstrance in French setting forth their grievances. Loudoun "returned it and said [he] could receive no memorial from the King's subjects but in English." In a meeting held to respond to Loudoun's action, the exiles "determined they would give no Memorial but in French." Infuriated by the Acadian response, Loudoun ordered the incarcerated Acadian leaders placed aboard the HMS *Sutherland*, a British warship bound for England.

The Pennsylvania Acadians nevertheless remained resolutely intransigent and insolent. They held public celebrations to mark French victories in the French and Indian War, and in 1761 they petitioned King George to redress their grievances against the Pennsylvania government. In 1761 they mounted a second effort to block a renewed attempt by the colonial government to bind out their children to Anglo artisans.

Other Acadian groups were less flamboyant, but all refused to submit without a struggle. In 1763, for example, after the Treaty of Paris ended the French and Indian War, the Acadian survivors in England made their way to France, where, for more than twenty years, they resisted French attempts to cast them in the mold of French peasants.

The resistance of Acadian exiles to oppression was not restricted to the exiles in the seaboard colonies, England, and France. A group of Acadians in the Beaubassin region avoided deportation by tunneling out of the post in which they were detained under armed guard. They later joined the resistance movement organized in present-day New Brunswick by the legendary Joseph Broussard *dit* Beausoleil. Broussard's forces not only threw back British military incursions into their settlement area, but his Acadians, in turn, raided British installations in Nova Scotia. They also procured letters of marque from the French Canadian governor and operated a privateer against British shipping. Broussard's resistance movement continued until late 1758, when the French military defeat at Louisbourg signaled the region's inevitable occupation by British forces.

A NEW ACADIA

Locked away in detention centers (concentration camps in modern parlance) at Halifax for the duration of the war, the members of the Acadian resistance were pressed into service as laborers on Nova Scotia's Acadian-designed and -constructed dike system, which the region's new Anglo colonists could not operate and maintain. Following their release, the Halifax Acadians requested permission to remain in the Bay of Fundy Basin. The Nova Scotian government refused. The Acadians then requested permission to settle in Quebec, where the large French population faced no immediate threat of assimilation.

This request was also denied. They then requested permission to establish themselves at St. Pierre and Miquelon, two small, windswept islands off the southern coast of Newfoundland, the only North American territory remaining in French possession. This request, too, was refused. The Halifax Acadians then pooled their resources and chartered a ship to carry them to Saint-Domingue (present-day Haiti), to which many exiles had been lured by French promises of assistance. Shortly before their departure, however, they received a letter from friends and relatives in Saint-Domingue warning of maltreatment by local French authorities. The Halifax group then determined to sail to Saint-Domingue, change ship, sail on to New Orleans, and ascend the Mississippi River to the Illinois Country, whence they intended to travel overland to Quebec.

They made it as far as New Orleans, where they encountered a bankrupt colonial government unable to provide them with much assistance. Under Broussard *dit* Beausoleil's leadership, the Halifax Acadians determined to remain in Louisiana in settlements they dubbed New Acadia. Established along Bayou Teche, they soon began to invite relatives and friends to join them in Louisiana and to assist them in raising a New Acadia from the ashes of the old. (They issued these invitations without awaiting the necessary governmental authorization.) The invitations struck responsive chords among the Acadian exiles in the Mid-Atlantic colonies and in France. Between 1766 and 1769 most of the Acadians remaining in Maryland and Pennsylvania sailed to Louisiana. They were followed in 1785 by approximately sixteen hundred Acadians from France. It is notable that the groups most active in resistance to outside oppression during the period of exile and wanderings congregated in Louisiana. It is also noteworthy that, in 1768, these recent Acadian immigrants participated in an armed uprising that drove from the province Louisiana's governor, who had forcibly dispersed the Acadian immigrants from Middle Atlantic colonies along the Mississippi River. It was certainly not coincidental that, when the 1785 Acadian immigrants arrived at New Orleans, they were allowed to settle wherever they pleased.

The Process of Adaptation

Recent studies suggest that the prevailing popular and scholarly images of Acadian immigration and settlement and the subsequent course of Acadian sociocultural evolution in Louisiana have little basis in fact. The bayou country was not an "Eden in Louisiana," as Longfellow and his successors have claimed, but a dense and forbidding semitropical jungle. The region's established residents did not welcome the exiles with open arms, as proponents of the Evangeline myth would have it. And, finally, the Acadian descendants of the destitute immigrants were not universally poor, dull-witted, church-dominated peons, as nineteenth- and early-twentieth-century travelers maintained. Instead, the Acadians constituted a complex society whose subregional differences were inadvertently preserved by the patterns of immigration and settlement.

Subregional differences, however, between Louisiana's Acadian communities were initially superficial, masking the shared values and basic lifestyle that bound the group together. Cohesiveness within Louisiana's various New Acadia settlements was bolstered by an extensive network of blood relationships. Internal unity was also fostered by painful encounters between the immigrants and rival groups, whose menacing presence constantly reminded the settlers of their vulnerability.

Deeply traumatized by the destruction of their homeland and the long years of exile preceding the founding of New Acadia, the Acadians initially became an insular society, consciously avoiding contact with rival groups to prevent assimilation. Although the walls of Acadian insularity were occasionally damaged, they were never effectively breached, and the core values of the Acadian immigrants were essentially those of their Acadian descendants.

The typical pre-dispersal Acadian cherished land, family, and personal dignity above all else. Having emigrated from France prior to the rise of capitalism, they were not materialistic in the modern sense of the term. Indeed, the Acadians sought only a comfortable existence, producing agricultural surpluses in order to acquire European manufactured goods to ameliorate their often harsh existence—never for conspicuous consumption.

These common values were perpetuated by the increasingly common endogamous marriages in seventeenth-century Acadian society and the resulting reinforcement of group boundaries. Group boundaries coincided with extended families, and, as the Acadian settlements were peopled primarily by the intermarried descendants of French colonial Acadia's remarkably prolific 1630s immigrants, the Acadian community did, in fact, constitute one large clan. This complex network of human relationships quickly became so tightly interwoven that, by 1700, the Acadians had come to consider themselves as a distinctive people. Indeed, the Acadians were the first European immigrant group to develop a distinctly North American identity.

Although it was a powerful influence in the Acadians' daily lives, the extended family never completely overwhelmed the individual. On the contrary, the Acadian frontiersman was fiercely individualistic. Producing all of the essentials of life himself—from food to clothing and shelter—the Acadian depended upon no one for his livelihood. As master of his modest farm, the Acadian frontiersman bowed to no man.

Nor would he brook any interference in his private affairs. As part of a culture born before the rise of modern European nationalism, he acknowledged allegiance first to his family and then to his native region. Europe was but a dim and rapidly fading memory. Thus, by 1700 the typical Acadian had come to view both the provincial government and the Catholic Church as merely necessary evils, tolerated solely for the basic services they provided. Any deviation from the parameters of accepted administrative functions was considered an unjustified encroachment on personal liberties and met with a swift and strongly negative response. Indeed, the Acadians demonstrated no hesitancy whatsoever in protesting to higher authorities the activities of their local secular and religious representatives. When active resistance proved unfeasible, the Acadians often foiled unpopular administrative programs through procrastination and by passive resistance. Faced by external pressure from a hostile, or at least unsympathetic, government, the Acadians drew upon their now mature group consciousness, formed a united front, and dealt with their antagonists only through popularly elected representatives.

The unshakable unity and basic cultural homogeneity of the Acadians permitted them to endure the trauma of the terrible diaspora of 1755. The cohesiveness of the Acadian exiles, which enabled them to maintain their identity throughout the long years of exile, permitted them to weather the rigors of establishing a new homeland—a new Acadia—in semitropical Louisiana. The region's warm and humid environment, nevertheless, quickly affected the nascent colony; scores, if not hundreds, of Acadians succumbed to epidemics of endemic fevers and other diseases. But, once acclimated to the climate, the exiles quickly adapted their diverse economic pursuits to the region's terrain, long growing season, and hot, humid temperatures. Moreover, as the various waves of Acadian immigrants were providentially placed on lands not dissimilar to those of their original Nova Scotian settlements, adaptation was correspondingly easy. It is thus hardly surprising that most Acadians attained their pre-dispersal standard of living within a decade of their arrival in Louisiana.

Although prosperity initially provided the exiles with sufficient economic independence to rebuild their world and pursue their own lifestyle, the steady accumulation of wealth over several decades by industrious Acadians presented the threat of rapid cultural disintegration. Economic stratification had existed in *vieille Acadie,* but wealth had not automatically endowed its owner with social position. In Louisiana's emerging slave society, however, accumulation of wealth, and particularly ownership of human chattel, automatically gave one social status.

First-generation Acadian immigrants remained unimpressed by the aristocratic trappings incumbent upon slave ownership, and, although some exiles acquired black field hands and wet nurses in the 1770s and 1780s, their simple, pastoral existence remained basically unaltered. But children and grandchildren in prosperous Acadian households also clearly envied the prestige enjoyed by their Creole neighbors and consciously attempted to alter their lifestyle to gain acceptance by their social "betters." Between the time of Louisiana's admission to the Union in 1812 and the beginning of the Civil War in 1861, upwardly mobile, second- and third-generation Louisiana Acadians increasingly modeled their existence upon that of the white Creole planter class, purchasing large numbers of slaves, engaging in large-scale staple crop production, building ostentatious homes, dabbling in thoroughbred horse racing, and educating their children in distant boarding schools. The most prosperous members of the emerging Acadian "establishment" also sought to marry their children into prominent Creole families.

Such cultural apostasy was atypical, although Acadian planters became more numerous in the original (colonial) Acadian settlement sites during the twilight years of the antebellum period. Throughout the early nineteenth century most Acadians preferred the less ostentatious existence of their forebears. Outside of the plantation areas only a small minority of Acadians owned slaves, and most landholders continued to engage in small-scale farming and ranching. In addition, the *petit habitant*'s (or yeoman farmer's) lodging remained the one- or two-room cottage developed in the 1760s and 1770s.

Pressures from the rapid evolution of southern Louisiana society nevertheless took their toll. Because of the early-nine-teenth-century exodus of Acadians who fled from local levee maintenance and the scarcity of available land in the bottom-land areas, the Acadians remaining along the Mississippi River and bayous Teche and Lafourche became socially and culturally isolated. Moreover, because their landholdings were gener-ally too small to engage in commercial agriculture as a result of Louisiana's forced heirship laws and because they usually lacked the funds to expand their farms, especially at inflation-ary antebellum land prices, many Acadians were compelled to abandon traditional agricultural pursuits in order to sur-vive economically. These Acadians found ready employment in the sugar industry as overseers, artisans, and laborers, but, hav-ing lost their economic independence, these workers became the first casualties of creeping Americanization in the region.

Further erosion of traditional Acadian life was accelerated by the outbreak of the Civil War. The growing sectional strife characterizing American politics in the late antebellum period and culminating in the nation's tragic fratricidal conflict had been of little interest to Louisiana's Acadians. Indeed, until the 1840s most Acadians, particularly the *petits habitants,* had preferred to shun politics altogether. But in the 1840s the grow-ing popularity of Jacksonian ideology, as articulated by the state's Democratic Party, coupled with Acadian Alexandre Mouton's emergence as the party's champion and ratification of the 1845 state constitution, which established universal white male suffrage, lured hundreds of previously apolitical Acadians into the Democratic camp. By the 1850s the Acadians had become the backbone of the Democratic Party in South Louisiana.

The political vision of these Democratic recruits commonly extended no farther than their respective parish boundaries. National politics thus initially held little appeal for Louisiana's Acadians. National issues, however, became increasingly difficult to ignore in the turbulent decade before the Civil War. State and local politicians used the emotional national questions of slavery and national unity to generate frenzied support for their respective parties at the numerous barbecues and rallies inevitably preceding Pelican State elections.

Among the most popular of the late antebellum stump speakers in southern Louisiana was former Governor Alexandre Mouton, whose fiery Southern Rights oratory did much to shape public opinion among poor Acadians regarding the nation's rapidly intensifying sectional confrontation. Therefore, while most Acadian planters voted for moderate Cooperationist candidates in the 1860 election, the vast majority of *petits habitants,* who looked to the Acadian community's elder statesman for political leadership, supported the secessionist ticket.

The pro-secessionist Acadian voters soon reaped a bitter harvest. Louisiana quickly joined its sister states of the Gulf South in severing their ties with the federal government, and civil warfare was the inevitable result. Acadians, however, were initially unaffected by the outbreak of hostilities, though many scions of Acadian planter families quickly volunteered for service in the Confederate army. As the South's military fortunes dimmed in 1862 and the fratricidal conflict assumed a regional focus, many *petits habitants* became the unwilling victims of Confederate conscription.

The resulting resentment for the Confederate government was further inflamed by the confiscation of Acadian livestock and grain by the Confederate army. Acadian conscripts consequently deserted their Confederate units whenever the rebel army retreated in the face of periodic Union invasions of South Louisiana. Free from their effective bondage in the army, the deserters greeted the invaders as liberators, but their cheers were soon replaced by grumbling as the men in blue proved as or more oppressive than their Confederate counterparts. Indeed, unlike the rebel army, which foraged in the fertile bayou country when necessary, the Union forces sought to destroy the region's agricultural bounty and thus deprive the enemy of a valuable supply base.

Consequently faced with starvation, the ever-present threat of destruction by the rival armies, and the possibility of arrest and execution for desertion, the Acadians were caught in a crossfire between distant powers. Once again, the Acadians were victimized by a cause that they generally did not espouse, witnessing the ruthless destruction of the fruit of their labors in the preceding decades, and, once again, their homeland lay in ashes.

The task of rebuilding was complicated not only by the political turbulence that plagued Louisiana between 1865 and 1877 but also by significant social and economic changes that accelerated the transformation of the transplanted Acadian society into the indigenous Louisiana Cajun culture. Class distinctions, which had emerged in the antebellum period, became more pronounced as the educated elite turned its back on its heritage altogether. They increasingly wished to avoid the onerous social stigma borne by those identified increasingly as "Cajuns" (an Anglo corruption of *Acadians*) in the postbellum period, the apparent result of much unfavorable publicity by the Northern popular press. Even the newly emancipated freedmen, who formerly constituted the doormat of local society, quickly came to view their Cajun neighbors with derision as they evidently reflected the anti-Cajun bigotry of their former masters.

Abandoned by the group's antebellum leadership element and under mounting pressure to conform to the Anglo-American norm, many Acadians found themselves ill equipped to meet the challenge of life in the postbellum South. Economically ruined by the war, some Acadians were forced to abandon their traditional agricultural pursuits and to seek their livelihoods—first as cypress lumberjacks and later as fishermen and trappers—in the Atchafalaya Basin and the coastal marshes. Many more were reduced to tenantry by the end of the nineteenth century. Those drawn into poverty soon discovered that they could not escape their predicament. They would remain mired in tenantry until the industrialization of Texas's "Golden Triangle" area in the first two decades of the twentieth century provided well-paying jobs to thousands of these impoverished people. Throughout the late nineteenth and early twentieth centuries the tenants' reduced circumstances forced them to interact daily with black fellow tenants—despite mounting pressure for segregation—and the resulting cultural interchanges helped produce both modern Cajun music and Cajun cuisine (as well as zydeco music in the black Creole community). Such interchanges, which were particularly numerous in the Eunice, Louisiana, area, helped to blur, at least in the eyes of outside observers, the long-standing cultural cleavages between the Acadians and their prairie Creole neighbors to the north. By the turn of the twentieth century these poor prairie Creoles, who, like the Acadians, had been abandoned by their own ethnic leadership element, gravitated economically and politically toward their southern, French-speaking neighbors, with whom they shared an increasingly common lifestyle. Indeed, the traditional prairie Creole settlement was designated

Evangeline Parish in 1910 in honor of its officially recognized, but appropriately mythical, Acadian heritage.

Poor Creoles east of the Atchafalaya River, and particularly in the Lafourche Basin, also adopted the Cajun identity as they became acculturated through intermarriage. Indeed, the assimilation of the eastern Creoles into the Lafourche Acadian community has been so complete that such families as the Quatrevingts (originally Achtzigger), Chauvins, Himels, Verrets, Cantrelles, and Haydels are generally unaware that their German and French ancestors arrived in Louisiana fully a half-century before the Acadians.

As with the lower strata of Acadian society, many members of the up-and-coming antebellum gentry were profoundly affected by the Civil War and its aftermath. The war itself claimed most of its prominent young politicians. Not until the turn of the century would the Acadian gentry begin to reassert a modicum of its notable antebellum influence on the regional and state levels.

Loss of political influence reflected a corresponding loss of economic power resulting from the ravages of Union invasions, Confederate foraging, vandalism by freedmen, and the postwar economic slump. Most severely impacted were those planters' children who grew to manhood just before, or during, the conflict. Unable to find a niche in agriculture, many of these young Acadians migrated to South Louisiana's farming villages, such as Vermilionville (present-day Lafayette), Plaquemine, and Thibodaux, where they emerged as a new professional class. Falling back on their classical educations, these urban Cajuns generally developed comfortable existences as sugar and cotton factors, attorneys, merchants, clerks, bill collectors, and educators.

This movement into the mercantile community held profound social and cultural ramifications for the Acadian upper class; in postbellum Acadiana, as in contemporary New Orleans, the language of business was English, and the Acadian social climbers who had formerly aspired to the social heights of Creole society now moved rapidly into the Anglo-American mainstream. Because of the social stigma now associated with less affluent Acadians, the Acadian gentry made every effort to disassociate itself from its heritage, initially wrapping itself instead in the ennobling mantle of the Evangeline legend and ultimately identifying itself as simply "American."

The children of these acculturated Acadians were in the vanguard of the early-twentieth-century movement to Americanize the Acadians. Focusing on public education as the best means of bringing the state's illiterate French speakers into the national mainstream, the movement was propelled by Louisiana's compulsory education act of 1916 and by the obligatory English educational provisions of the 1921 state constitution. Although the authors of these laws were Anglos, most of

the teachers who implemented the English instructional program were drawn from the Acadian gentry class. These teachers showed no more sympathy than their Anglo colleagues for
Cajun French, and French speakers in their care were chastised
and publicly humiliated for using their mother tongue on the
school grounds.

The frontal assault on Cajun French by the state's educational establishment was complemented by technological, social, and economic developments that more effectively undermined the language by discouraging its use at home. The
appearance of movies, radio programming, and other popular
new forms of entertainment, all of which were available exclusively in English, encouraged monolingual French Cajuns to
become fully bilingual. Meanwhile, Louisiana's burgeoning oil
industry, run by English-speaking Texans and Oklahomans, provided unprecedented employment opportunities in Acadiana
but only for those Cajuns with at least a moderate degree of
fluency in English. A Cajun driller, for example, made more
than four times as much as a local sharecropper. To provide
their children with the opportunity for a better standard of
living than they themselves had enjoyed, many working-class
Cajun parents began to use English exclusively when convers-
ing with their children; this is particularly true of those Cajuns who had experienced the trauma of adapting to the
English-only educational regime.

The threatened demise of the French language jeopardized other cultural institutions including Cajun music, which, in the mid-1930s and early 1940s, saw the introduction of western swing and country music styles and the increasing use of English. In addition, the introduction of mechanization and electrification around World War II obviated the need for both the traditional communal harvest (kept alive by manpower shortages during the war) and the *boucherie* (communal country butchery), and both virtually disappeared by 1960. These institutions, together with the *veillées,* or regular evening visits with neighbors and relatives, had served to renew group bonds. With the emergence of television in the late 1950s and early 1960s, moreover, these visits became less and less frequent, and, ultimately, they too passed from the scene.

Few mourned the passing of these activities, for Louisiana's Acadian population had embarked upon a seemingly irreversible march into the American mainstream. The mainstream offered promise of the good life, and those elements of their cultural baggage popularly associated with their heritage were denigrated as archaic, crude ("low class"), or absurd. The very term *Cajun,* for example, came, by the late 1950s, to be viewed as the supreme insult to persons of French descent in Acadiana, and use of this "epithet" often produced a strongly negative, if not violent, response. Rejection of the past was also manifested in more subtle ways, including naming practices. Children born to Cajun parents between the onset of the Great Depression and the end of the Baby Boom generation were generally christened with given names deemed typically "American"—particularly Anglo or Irish surnames such as Brent, Murphy, and Barry— to facilitate their passage into the materialistic promised land.

Survival in the mainstream, however, required a broad range of educational and occupational skills that the blue-collar parents themselves could not provide. Having gained an appreciation for education through their participation in Civilian Conservation Corps (CCC) camps or during military service during World War II, these parents, like their opposite numbers throughout the nation, stressed education as the key to financial success in the 1950s and 1960s. Indeed, young Cajuns were pressured to attend college, and the student populations at southern Louisiana universities doubled in size during this period. The resulting wave of Cajun college graduates tended to congregate in the college towns, where they came to constitute a notable segment of Acadiana's urban population.

Unlike their counterparts of the preceding century, however, these upwardly mobile, urban Cajuns did not abandon their parent culture entirely. Indeed, like members of other minorities throughout the United States, many urban Cajuns found that their Anglo-Protestant neighbors simply would not let them forget their past, and many others became deeply disillusioned with homogenization into the great, rootless American mass.

These young Cajun urbanites, in the late 1960s and early 1970s, came to resent the fact that they had ever been made to feel ashamed of their heritage.

The resulting backlash contributed to the establishment of the Council for the Development of French in Louisiana (COD-OFIL) in 1968. Under the leadership of former Congressman Jimmie Domengeaux, CODOFIL articulated this long-suppressed resentment and, in doing so, did much to rehabilitate the Cajuns' self-image. By the early 1970s placards in business places throughout southern Louisiana proclaimed, for the first time since World War II, "Ici on parle français [We speak French here]."

Although centered in Lafayette, the self-proclaimed cultural capital of Acadiana and home of the largest urban Cajun community, this ethnic revival was by no means an urban, white-collar phenomenon. By the early 1970s the movement enjoyed the unspoken popular endorsement of blue-collar groups that had traditionally been the main cultural guardians. Their renewed sense of pride and their disdain for those Cajuns who had only recently come out of the closet were brought home quite graphically in the early 1970s, when members of this group began to identify themselves as "coonasses"—a term of disputed origin which had replaced *Cajun* as the ultimate local epithet in the 1960s—much to the horror of the "genteel" Acadians. Indeed, in the early 1970s many blue-collar Cajuns began to sport

T-shirts and bumper stickers identifying themselves as "proud coonasses."

Blue-collar Cajun attitudes are particularly significant because of the group's tremendous growth, relative to the other segments of the Cajun population, over the past thirty years. The rise of this socioeconomic group was tied directly to recent developments in the oil industry. Following the 1973 oil embargo, the Louisiana petroleum industry experienced an unprecedented growth spurt. The expansion created a tremendous demand for skilled blue-collar workers, particularly welders, pipe fitters, roustabouts, mud engineers, and drillers. Salaries for these positions rose dramatically, reflecting the current market conditions. A welder made approximately twice the salary, for example, of a high school principal. Recognizing this, thousands of teenage Cajuns abandoned the classroom for the job market, and by 1980 Louisiana led the nation in the number of high school dropouts.

Although the short-term benefits of such actions were high, the long-term costs to the Cajun community, and to the state as a whole, were great as well. The regional oil depression, which began in December 1985, left most of the blue-collar workforce without employment, and the presence of a large reservoir of poorly educated workers only perpetuated Louisiana's long-standing national reputation for backwardness. This image has, in turn, discouraged desirable, non-petroleum-related industries from moving into the area, thereby retarding diversification of southern Louisiana's economy. Indeed, despite favorable reviews of Lafayette's potential as an "aspiring high-tech mecca" in national computer publications and the construction of a high-tech industrial park near the Hub City's northside in the late 1980s, the "silicon bayou" failed to attract any major high-tech concerns.

Faced with bleak prospects of short-term improvement in the local economy and burdened with straitened personal finances, many unemployed Cajuns began, in 1986, to relocate in Tennessee, Georgia, and Florida, where jobs were more abundant. The actual number of emigrants was estimated in the tens of thousands. When coupled with the outpouring of immigrant oil workers, the Cajun exodus was sufficient for local truck rental dealerships to place a surcharge on vehicles leaving Acadiana. In fact, the number of transplanted Cajuns in Atlanta was reportedly sufficiently large to prompt the creation of an anti-Cajun bumper sticker stating, "Cajuns Go Home."

The blue-collar exodus was followed by the out-migration of large numbers of Cajun college graduates throughout the final decade of the twentieth century and the first early years of the twenty-first. Most of these recent emigrants have settled either in Texas, particularly Houston, Dallas–Fort Worth, and Austin, or along the West Coast. The white- and blue-collar diasporas, reminiscent of the Cajun migration to the Golden

Triangle area of the early twentieth century, will almost certainly result in the complete assimilation of the emigrants into the American mainstream.

But what of those who stayed behind? A majority of Louisiana's Cajuns have remained in Acadiana, and, like their Acadian immigrant ancestors, they face major challenges to both their culture and their economic way of life. Cajun French is particularly threatened. Interest in the language, as well as the bilingual programs established after 1968 to perpetuate it, began to wane sometime before 1980, particularly on the grassroots level, in response to CODOFIL's unpopular importation of foreign nationals to teach metropolitan French to Louisiana schoolchildren. Because of apathy, and in some areas open hostility, toward bilingual education among the Cajuns themselves, some area school boards began to curtail French classes in the early 1980s. The economic crisis of the mid-1980s caused further retrenchment. The establishment of immersion programs in various southern Louisiana parishes in the 1990s occasioned renewed optimism, but only approximately two thousand students participated, far less than the critical mass needed to make the language self-sustaining. Hence, the future of Cajun French is at best uncertain.

Also in a state of flux is the traditional Cajun adherence to the Roman Catholic Church. The Acadians have maintained strong anticlerical tendencies since their colonization in Canada, and these anticlerical biases, coupled with a strong backlash against post–Vatican II changes, the Church's role in integration and opposition to birth control, and growing impersonalization in the urban areas have propelled thousands of Cajun Catholics into the myriad fundamentalist sects that have sprung up in Acadiana since 1970. Indeed, fundamentalist churches have enjoyed a growth rate approximately twenty times that of the natural increase in the local population.

Other facets of Cajun culture, however, have remained robust. The cohesiveness of nuclear families persists, and the extended family, while not the force that it once was in Acadian society, nevertheless remains the mortar that holds the Cajun community together. Cajun cuisine and Cajun music—the latter on the verge of disappearing around World War II— are now the subject of national fascination and will endure for some time, if only for economic reasons. The Cajun proclivity for getting the most out of life, a trait grossly distorted by the popular media, remains a necessary counterbalance to their traditional fatalism and the monotony of their long and arduous workweeks. Cajuns have also maintained not only a strong appreciation for their natural surroundings but also a deepseated attachment to their Louisiana homeland. Although modern economic realities have also forced them to surrender their traditional self-sufficiency, they have nevertheless maintained their spirit of independence and irreverence toward all forms of authority.

Yet the Cajuns find themselves at a crossroads: the cultural gap between subregional groups, between urbanites and country folk, and, indeed, between generations continues to grow. It is consequently difficult to make generalizations. One thing, however, is clear: the Cajuns themselves—not external influences or forces—will make the ultimate decision about the course of their community's ongoing cultural and linguistic evolution.

CHAPTER THREE

Creoles: A Family Portrait in
Black and White

*Clever men are impressed in their differences from
their fellows. Wise men are conscious of their resem-
blances to them.*

R. H. Tawney

LOUISIANA'S BEAUTIFUL SEMITROPICAL LAND-
scape and unique cultural environment annually lure millions
of tourists to the Bayou country. The region's French-speaking
inhabitants constitute perhaps the most important ingredient
in the state's exotic mystique. To the visitor these "strange" people are shrouded in obscurity as seemingly impenetrable and
mysterious as the swamps and marshes that border their settlements.

Native-born Louisianians of French descent unfortunately
often know as little about their own background as the tourists

who visit them. As a result of the denigration of the state's Francophone communities by the popular media throughout much of the nineteenth and twentieth centuries, the scholarly community took little note of the poor, "benighted" denizens of America's great backwater. The problem was compounded by the deplorable quality of what little published material did exist. A 1984 survey by the Council for the Development of French in Louisiana (CODOFIL) discovered that Edwin Adams Davis's *Louisiana, the Pelican State,* then the most widely utilized Louisiana history textbook, contained only two paragraphs on the Acadians: the first included a distillation of Henry Wadsworth Longfellow's *Evangeline,* while the second announced the imminent demise of the Cajun community. Davis provided even less information regarding Creoles. Other contemporary works providing more ample coverage of the state's Francophone peoples were generally no better. Written primarily by laymen, these works contained roughly equal portions of fact and fantasy. (Louisianians, of course, have never been known to let the facts stand in the way of a good story.)

Louisiana Studies and Francophone Studies scholars have done much to correct this deficiency over the past two decades, but most of the new scholarship has focused on a single group—the Cajuns. Until very recently, this has tended to mask the great cultural, racial, and ethnic diversity in Louisiana's French-speaking region, an area that ethnographers have come to regard in recent years as the home of North America's most complex rural society.

This complexity stands in stark contrast with the simplistic, racist stereotypes foisted on an unsuspecting world by Hollywood and the electronic media. It is thus hardly surprising that outsiders have tended to view French-speaking Louisianians as a monolithic group sharing a common background. There are, however, more than a dozen distinct French-speaking groups in Louisiana, and they have all played a significant role in the state's development. These groups arrived in Louisiana at different times and under different circumstances over the past three centuries. Twentieth-century Louisiana, for example, witnessed the arrival of French-speaking Lebanese Christians, Vietnamese, Laotians, and Haitians as well as numerous French and Belgian war brides and CODOFIL-recruited French, Belgian, Quebecois, and Acadian teachers. Each group has a distinctive historical, social, or economic background that sets it apart from neighboring French-speaking groups in Louisiana. Indeed, differences among these groups were often as significant as those presently dividing national and ethnic groups on the European continent or, indeed, between Northeasterners and Southerners in the United States.

Over time interaction between Louisiana's different Francophone communities and the cultural borrowing that it engendered transformed all of the cultural groups involved in the exchange. A key player in this exchange was the Creole community—once itself the focal point of historical, linguistic, and cultural studies of French Louisiana but relegated to the slag heap of late-twentieth-century historiography. The past twelve years, however, have seen a revival in scholarly interest, witnessed by the publication of nine major works on Louisiana Creoles—six of which were published between 1992 and 1997. Despite this flurry of recent publishing activity, no one has attempted a comprehensive look at the development of Louisiana's remarkably complex and diverse Creole community, producing in effect a family portrait in black and white.

The word *Creole* itself simply means native or indigenous to an area, but over the years the term has gained a multiplicity of meanings, as different groups have ascribed the label to various distinct peoples. The resulting confusion, both within the state and throughout the country, is such that the most commonly asked question in Louisiana Studies is "what does the term *Creole* mean?" Its usage has evolved over the years, and the term consequently has come to mean something different to virtually everyone using it.

The word *Creole* is a French corruption of the Spanish term *criollo.* Historian Joseph Tregle, citing Garcilaso de la Vega, maintains that the term was "invented by the Negroes" who used it to distinguish American-born slaves from bondsmen born in Guinea. This claim is affirmed by recent scholarship demonstrating that the term *criollo* was in common usage in the Spanish New World settlements as early as the 1560s and that the word was reserved exclusively for slaves. Usage of the term changed over the two ensuing centuries. In South America, native-born whites eventually came to apply the term exclusively to themselves. In the sugar islands, on the other hand, the term *Creole* was applied to natives of all racial backgrounds.

In Saint-Domingue, established by the French on the western end of formerly Spanish Hispaniola, *Creole* meant native-born "without reference to color." This usage was transplanted to Louisiana, which was established shortly after Saint-Domingue. White and black Louisiana natives were consistently identified as Creoles in extant eighteenth-century census reports, ship lists, judicial records, ecclesiastical registers, muster rolls, and administrative correspondence. In early Louisiana the term meant the descendants of pioneers—French, Spanish, German, Irish, Italian, sometimes even English, and African—who were born in the region prior to the Louisiana Purchase. When applied to whites, the word initially carried a derogatory connotation, for newly arrived European colonists, both in the Spanish and French colonies, considered themselves inherently superior to their American-born neighbors, whose brains, they believed, were addled by the tropical sun. Over the years, however, a common culture, economic pursuits, and a high degree of intermarriage transformed these Louisiana-born progeny of Europeans into a caste that generally considered itself superior to other French-speaking groups in the state, particularly the Acadians. Thus, the term *Creole* became synonymous with *aristocrat,* and today, when white Louisianians of French ancestry call themselves Creole, what they really mean is that they are not Cajuns, a group that they traditionally considered "white trash." (Although technically Creoles, the eighteenth- and nineteenth-century Cajuns, recoiling from the local gentry's social pretensions, refused to apply the term to themselves. Only members of the Acadian elite publicly assumed a Creole identity, and then usually for political expediency.)

The term *Creole* was not applied exclusively to the progeny of European pioneers. In colonial and antebellum Louisiana white Creoles coexisted with black Creoles. Native-born slaves generally carried a significantly higher price tag than freshly imported Africans or West Indians because they were considered to be more docile, seasoned to the climate, trained for field work or domestic tasks, and, most important, French-speaking. Numerous Creole slaves were manumitted in the late eighteenth and early nineteenth centuries. Their descendants, the *gens de couleur libres* (free persons of color), would eventually identify themselves as Creoles, much to the horror of the white Creole community.

Closely related to the noun *Creole* (capital *C*) is the adjective *creole* (lowercase *c*), which refers to the adaptation of a product to a New World environment. Thus, in Louisiana there were creole ponies (a breed that probably no longer exists), creole tomatoes, and creole onions.

Creole is also used to denote a speaker of a Creole language. Creole dialects arise in areas where two languages come into contact, one the tongue of a dominant elite, often masters in a slave society, the other the speech of a dominated mass, usually slaves. Creole dialects begin as a *pidgin,* a greatly simplified, hybrid version of the dominant language, intermingled with words and phrases from the other, subordinate tongue. A pidgin enables each group to communicate with the other while continuing to use its own speech. When a pidgin totally displaces either or both languages instead of coexisting with them, it becomes a "Creole" dialect. In the New World there are English, Dutch, and French Creole dialects. In Louisiana the term *Creole* can thus refer to black and mixed-race speakers of the French Creole dialect, much to the white Creoles' chagrin. This affront to white Creole pride, however, elicited a far milder reaction than postbellum suggestions that European ancestry was not the sole criterion for membership in Louisiana's Creole fraternity. In fact, George Washington Cable, a nationally prominent writer of the late nineteenth century, was literally run out of New Orleans for suggesting in his works that blacks could also be called "Creoles." This attitude persists in some quarters, and the subject remained sufficiently controversial in

New Orleans to spawn a documentary called *The Creole Controversy* in the late 1980s.

WHITE CREOLES

This multiplicity of meanings leads to considerable confusion. The term *Creole* often varies in meaning depending on who is speaking and what is spoken about. But in Louisiana it is in the cultural sense that *Creole* is used most frequently, and the term conjures up images of grandeur and glamour, of columned plantation houses, filled with mahogany furniture, expensive crystal, and fine silverware. The stereotypical Creole aristocrat's house was, of course, supported by armies of field hands and legions of domestic servants. Creole women, the stereotype goes, were always beautiful, graceful, gracious, sophisticated, and high-spirited; the men, handsome, proud to the point of arrogance, and brave to the point of recklessness. As a Creole character in a George Washington Cable short story tells his grandson: "Remember child, you belong to a race that has never bowed to man or God." Another writer, latter-day New Orleans Creole Launcelot Minor Harris, would have us believe that the Creole pioneers of St. Martinville "maintained the etiquette, and, as far as possible, the dress of the French court life." Still another New Orleans Creole, Joseph Tregle, a former history professor and dean of Liberal Arts at the University of New Orleans, however, paints a less idyllic portrait of his ancestors:

Provincial in outlook, style, and taste, the typical Latin Creole was complaisant, unlettered, unskilled, content to occupy his days with the affairs of his estate or the demands of his job, for it should be obvious that the average Creole was no more wealthy than the average man anywhere and worked where work was to be had. He lived in sensation rather than reflection, enjoying the balls and dances, betting heavily at table or perhaps at the cockpit, endlessly smoking his inevitable cigar, whiling away hours over his beloved dominoes, busying himself with the many demands of his close-knit family life. Seldom a fashion plate, he was more often than not adorned in pantaloons of blue cottonade, coarse and ungainly in appearance and separated from misshapen shoes by a considerable visible stretch of blue-striped yarn stockings. A hat of no standard style and an ill-fitted coat with long, narrow collars . . . usually completed the costume.

Tregle's observations constitute a drastic departure from the traditional stereotype, so much so that he seems to be speaking about a different group entirely. What, then, were the Louisiana Creoles, and which of these conflicting views best depicts their station in society? Was the typical Creole truly a member of a cultured aristocracy? Or was he or she an average person of modest means, hiding behind the facade of an intricate local mythology? The truth appears to lie somewhere between the polar extremes.

White Creole society was shaped by the French crucible in which it was formed. Louisiana was colonized by France at a time when French colonial policy dictated that colonies should be extensions of the mother country, literally "New Frances." Colonies were to have the same administrative institutions as the French provinces, be ministered to by the same church, and develop the same feudalistic social structure, with proper subordination of the lower classes to the "better elements of society." In these New Frances existing across the Atlantic, this highly structured society would consist—in the colonial ministry's vision—of whites at the top of the hierarchy, a peasantry consisting of converted Indians, and, in the case of Louisiana (and the sugar islands), an additional underclass of black serfs. This social system was to be established by the colonial governments through land grants and other privileges lavished upon the noble and wealthy classes and dispensed in a miserly fashion to lesser freemen.

The administrative architects of colonial Louisiana saw this new social order as an improved facsimile of France's anachronistic feudal society, precisely because of the more perfect regimentation of the lower classes. Although the *philosophes* might praise the independence, or, more to the point, the insubordination, of Indian warriors vis-à-vis their chiefs, most eighteenth-century Frenchmen, living under an absolutist monarchy, saw the lack of a powerful ruling class as proof of the

Indians' savagery. In fact, throughout the eighteenth century Frenchmen in Louisiana universally referred to Native Americans as *les sauvages* (savages).

Given this mentality, it is easy to see how those colonists who carved a new home along the Mississippi River and the Gulf Coast would come to view themselves as the nucleus of an emerging colonial aristocracy. Status meant everything in Louisiana, as it did in France—one simply was regarded as what one appeared to be. From the earliest days of the colony, when chronic food and supply shortages threatened the very existence of the Louisiana settlement, the colonists fought constantly among themselves, not over food, clothing, or shelter, as one might expect, but over socially advantageous marriages, the location of their pews in church, and which officers' ranks took precedence over others when lining up for religious and governmental processions.

The jockeying for position then occurring between officials paled by comparison to the vicious rivalries between the colony's women. In 1704 one of the prospective brides sent to Louisiana refused to marry beneath her station, and not even France's minister of the Navy and Colonies could make her change her mind. These socially conscious Frenchwomen transferred their values to their children, the first generation of white Creoles in Louisiana. A good example of this is the Chauvin family. The first generation of Chauvins—three brothers—were

Canadian adventurers, backwoodsmen who came to Louisiana with Iberville at the dawn of Louisiana colonization. Two of them married Frenchwomen, while the third married a relative of Governor Bienville. Through hard work the Chauvin brothers managed to build some of the largest plantations along the Mississippi River, and their wealth earned them grudging recognition from the colony's French-born administrators: Nicolas Chauvin, though unlettered, served on the colony's court of last resort, the Superior Council, for many years before his death. The aspirations of the Chauvins, however, were not merely political, and it was perhaps through their wives' influence that the Canadians followed the example of the Le Moynes and other prominent Canadian families in using the particle *de* and a place name (e.g., Deléry) to distinguish branches of the family—as the French nobility would have done—instead of using *dit* names (nicknames), as was commonplace among the lower classes throughout the empire.

In a continuing effort to have the family take its proper station in Louisiana society, Nicolas Chauvin de Lafrénière, *fils,* son of the Superior Council member, was sent to France for an education superior to that of the Frenchmen then governing the colony. As a consequence, when he returned to Louisiana in 1763, bearing a royal commission as attorney general, he was able to establish himself as a force to be reckoned with in government and the spokesman for the interests of his fellow Creoles. It was in the latter capacity that he would devote most of his time and attention.

Lafrénière's role in the 1768 New Orleans rebellion is famous, but less well known is the part that he played in the evolution of the colony's slave system. In the 1750s and early 1760s Louisiana planters had come to view their slaves as an increasingly significant threat to the colony's internal security. Consequently, as one of his first acts after returning from France, Lafrénière began to use his judicial authority to tighten the relatively lax existing regulations on Louisiana slaves and thus moved to bring Louisiana into line with the prevailing French obsession with hierarchical control of the lower, subservient elements of society.

Tighter controls over slaves placed additional de facto power in the hands of the wealthy Creole farmers, who were by the late eighteenth century almost exclusively slaveholders. This, in turn, elevated the Creoles into the top social position in the emerging plantation areas along the Mississippi River, where they constituted a majority of the free population.

Thus, by 1770 the Creole caste, outside of New Orleans, had come to view itself as the aristocracy—and indeed it was—in Louisiana's poor mirror image of French society. Their self-image was given some credibility when many officers in Louisiana's French garrison retired and settled in the colony after 1763. Although only a handful of these former officers—DeClouet,

De L'Homme, Dauterive, and Delahoussaye—asserted a legitimate claim to nobility, and then only as chevaliers, the absolute lowest rung of the French nobility, several others were chevaliers of the Military Order of St. Louis, an honorific, nonhereditary title bestowed upon deserving officers for at least twenty years of meritorious service. Although their titles would have been sneered at in the mother country, they were highly prized in the backwater that was rural lower Louisiana. Dozens of chevaliers, in full dress uniform, still glare down upon their descendants in drawing rooms throughout southern Louisiana.

The pretensions of the rural Creoles were matched, and perhaps even surpassed, by those of their New Orleans cousins. New Orleans society prior to 1800 was nothing like what emerged after the Louisiana Purchase. The town was populated primarily by businessmen, and, as mercantile pursuits were off-limits to the French nobility, the town's businessmen had few social pretensions. But in 1809 approximately ten thousand refugees from the Haitian revolution, who had spent ten years growing sugarcane at Santiago de Cuba, arrived en masse, unannounced, at New Orleans' doorstep and immediately overwhelmed the native French-speaking population. Forced to leave their homes with little notice for the second time in a decade, they arrived with little more than what they could carry and the few domestic slaves who chose to follow them. These people, like those of southern Louisiana, had been farmers, and the social elite of their native communities. And, like the French elite, they considered commerce as being beneath their dignity, unless it was conducted on a massive, international scale, yet, lacking the resources to return to farming, they were trapped in the region's commercial center. Often highly educated, the Antillean Creoles utilized their skills to procure gainful employment in government, in the legal and medical professions, and as educators. Others rented their domestics to members of the Crescent City's native Creole community to make a living, while still others turned to journalism, operating the city's first newspapers. Finally, some refugees established theaters to sate the refugees' passionate love for French opera and ballet. No matter their economic status, the transplanted former French colonists put on their finest and went to the various theaters for weekend performances. Their continuing patronage of the theatrical and operatic arts helped to bring the country some of the finest European talent, and New Orleans became a center of classical culture in North America until the Civil War.

It was this love of theatricals, combined with their preoccupation with social status, which prompted the refugees, now the stereotypical New Orleans Creoles, to transform the Crescent City carnival from a drunken riot into its present form, with all of its pageantry and royalty. The attitudes that gave Mardi Gras its character, however, doomed the New Orleans Creoles to the status of a permanent economic underclass for the nineteenth century and much of the early twentieth century. Because their values permitted them to engage in only the "noble" professions—farming, the legal and medical professions, educational and governmental service—the Creoles permitted Anglo-American and European immigrants of the nineteenth century to move into, and quickly dominate, the city's thriving commercial sector. With wealth came status and political power. The New Orleans Creoles attempted to preserve their privileged niche in New Orleans society by establishing themselves as a city within a city. The Vieux Carré became a separate entity as New Orleans was divided into three municipalities, each governed by an autonomous city administration for much of the early nineteenth century.

Such isolationism only compounded the Creoles' problems, for it left the French Quarter, the heart of Creole New Orleans, with a very small tax base. City services consequently declined, as did the quality of life in the Vieux Carré, and it is precisely because of this pervasive poverty that the Quarter's old buildings were preserved. By the end of Reconstruction (1877) the French Quarter was a glorified slum. In fact, recent studies have shown that it was the decline in living standards in the Vieux Carré which forced the dispersal of New Orleans' Creole community in the early twentieth century. By the time of the 1905 yellow fever epidemic this glorified ghetto was filled with Sicilian immigrants—and, according to Board of Health officials, their goats. Dispersal of the Creole population was followed by rapid and near total assimilation.

The fate of the New Orleans Creoles was shared by their country cousins. Although blessed with greater economic opportunities, the country Creoles' values prevented them from acquiring the wealth that was within their grasp. Because of the importance of maintaining appearances, country Creoles used the profits from their agricultural endeavors to buy expensive silverware, carriages, rosewood or mahogany furniture, fine clothing; to retain dance instructors for their daughters; to commission fine portraits of themselves; to erect small, but ostentatious homes—in a word, for conspicuous consumption. Because little capital was reinvested in the farm, the overwhelming majority of Creoles never progressed beyond the level of small planters. The much ballyhooed stories of Valcour Aime notwithstanding, statistical analyses of the entire southern Louisiana region show clearly that of the three existing groups of planters—Anglo-Americans, Acadians/Cajuns, and Creoles— the Creoles were easily the least affluent members of southern Louisiana's gentry class. (The German Coast and Pointe Coupée Parish were notable exceptions to this general rule.)

The marginal economic status of the rural Creoles made them vulnerable to the economic depression that followed in the wake of the Civil War. Many planters, particularly those whose plantations were damaged or destroyed by fighting dur-

ing the war, lost everything after 1865. Generally poorly educated, the children of these planters found themselves with few
resources and quickly lost status, as they were forced to take any
job available to survive. This is also true of the metropolitan Creoles, who came to dominate clerical positions in the local re-
tail sales and banking industries.

The Creoles' fall from grace gave rise to a body of mythology regarding a golden age that never was. Most southern
Louisianians are familiar with the stories of the spiders imported from China for the Oak and Pine Alley wedding, with the
celebrated performances of French opera companies in antebellum St. Martinville, with the presence of the great houses of
French nobility who took refuge along Bayou Teche after the
French Revolution, and with the donation of a baptismal font
by Louis XVI to St. Martin of Tours Catholic Church—all stories proven unfounded by recent historical research. Yet these
stories persist because they gave, and still provide, the fallen
Creole elite with a continuing sense of social prominence based
upon perceived past glories.

This was absolutely necessary, the Creoles believed, to avoid
social leveling with the Acadians, who had, from their eighteenth-century arrival in Louisiana, steadfastly resisted the
efforts of Creoles to treat them like peasants, and with those
"other" white Creoles—the poor white Creoles that the genteel
Creoles never mentioned in polite society, except, of course,

as objects of ridicule. The most prominent elements of the poor white Creole community were the descendants of either French colonial enlisted men and yeomen or the Malagueño and Isleño immigrants of the late eighteenth century. Settled in the New Iberia, Plattenville, Port Vincent, Barataria, and Terre aux Boeufs areas, most of these Spanish immigrants, with the exception of those settled along Bayou Lafourche and in St. Bernard Parish, quickly lost their cultural identity and were absorbed by their Acadian neighbors. Those Bayou Lafourche and St. Bernard area Spaniards who proved more resistant to change adopted economic pursuits—fishing and trapping—which were deemed demeaning by genteel Creoles. Hence, neither group, while technically Creole, has ever identified itself as such, nor have they ever been claimed as *confrères* by the more affluent Creoles.

Nor have the genteel Creoles demonstrated any interest in their poor prairie relations. The prairie Creoles, like the genteel Creoles, are descendants of French colonists who were in Louisiana before the arrival of the Acadians. These people—the Fontenots, Lafleurs, Guillorys, Brignacs, Bonins, Laviolettes, and others—were originally settlers of the present state of Alabama before 1763. Most had been enlisted men in the Fort Toulouse garrison (located near present-day Montgomery, Alabama) until the English occupied the area in 1764. These former soldiers, and a few residents of Mobile, then migrated to settlement sites near present-day Washington, Louisiana, from which they quickly migrated to modern-day Evangeline Parish. There they became small farmers and ranchers very much like the Acadians residing only a few miles to the south, in present-day Acadia Parish. The resulting confusion among outsiders over prairie Creole identity is seen most clearly in the creation of Evangeline Parish in 1910, when the state legislature dubbed the region—populated primarily by prairie Creoles—Evangeline Parish in recognition of the population's appropriately mythical Acadian heritage.

There were nevertheless significant cultural differences between white prairie Creoles and their Acadian/Cajun neighbors, and the evidence clearly indicates that ethnic antagonisms existed between these groups. These differences were sometimes manifested in violent clashes, such as the Civil War raids upon Acadian communities by prairie Creole jayhawkers. Nor would these entrenched ethnic antagonisms fade rapidly. Indeed, contacts between prairie Creoles and prairie Cajuns in the twentieth century often erupted in violence, be it at high school football stadiums or at nightclubs. Even today the residents of Mamou will tell you privately that they "are not really Cajuns." But in recent years white prairie Creoles have nevertheless adopted the Cajun identity, partly to attract the tourist dollar and partly because the genteel Creoles' refusal to acknowledge them left them with no other acceptable French identity to which they could cling. (To identify themselves as Creole would inevitably entail confusion with the persons of mixed racial background who now call themselves Creoles of Color or, more commonly in recent years, simply Creole.)

The resulting blurring of cultural boundaries between Acadians/Cajuns and white prairie Creoles has given rise to a sharp increase in intermarriage between the two groups over the last three decades. This trend suggests an eventual complete merger of identities under the Cajun ethnic umbrella.

Like the white prairie Creoles, the Creoles of Color have suffered a major identity crisis in recent years. Creoles of Color are primarily descendants of the *gens de couleur libres,* those blacks who were free before the Civil War. Free blacks were present in Louisiana in the 1720s, though not in significant numbers until after the 1729–30 Natchez Wars, when scores of African slaves who had fought Indians alongside the French were rewarded with their freedom. Other slaves were emancipated for faithful service or because they had borne children of white farmers. In 1763 the free blacks numbered approximately 150 in a colonial population of about 10,000. Forty years later there were between 2,000 and 2,500 free blacks in Louisiana, and the growth of this group stemmed less from a natural increase than from the manumission of the mistresses and natural children of planters. Because manumissions became increasingly rare after the Americans assumed control of Louisiana, these free blacks formed the nucleus of a culturally and economically significant caste that would give Louisiana society its Caribbean character.

Enjoying most of the legal rights extended to whites, these former slaves became, in the nineteenth century, one of the most prosperous segments of Louisiana's free population. Usually labeled "mulattoes" by whites, despite a tremendous range in the racial mixture of individual group members, the *gens de couleur libres* congregated in small communities in the following areas before the Civil War: Isle Brevelle, near Natchitoches; the Leonville and Lawtell-Swords-Plaisance areas of St. Landry Parish; the Grand Marais area of present-day Iberia Parish; with smaller, less well-defined communities in Avoyelles, Iberville, and Vermilion parishes. Of these communities the St. Landry group was clearly the largest, consisting of 1,500 individuals in an 1860 population of approximately 21,500 (including 10,000 whites and 10,000 African-American slaves). But not all free blacks were rural people; the 1850 census of Vermilionville (present-day Lafayette), for example, indicates that 39 percent of the town's free population was composed of *les gens de couleur libres.*

The free black communities of antebellum southern Louisiana were composed primarily of artisans and craftsmen. In Vermilionville mulatto carpenters, blacksmiths, and joiners often owned property valued in excess of that possessed by most white farmers in the immediate vicinity of town. In southwestern Louisiana most of the antebellum hotels and many of the bordellos were owned and operated by free black women. Outside of towns, most free blacks were small farmers, and many owned slaves. A not insignificant number of mulattoes in St. Landry and Natchitoches parishes owned large numbers of slaves.[1] According to the 1840 census, for example, Martin Donato, a free man of color in St. Landry Parish, was one of the five largest slaveholders in Louisiana. Free black planters such as Donato and the Metoyers in Natchitoches Parish also served as private bankers to their white neighbors.

The urban free blacks shared in the waxing economic fortunes of their country counterparts. The free black community of New Orleans, which numbered approximately 19,000 out of a total population of about 150,000 in 1850, consisted principally of artisans and craftsmen, as in the rural towns. Particularly prominent were the ironworkers, who fashioned the beautiful iron grillwork that presently graces many buildings in the French Quarter. The free blacks also dominated the Crescent City docks for decades and were generally known as the most industrious longshoremen available in the Crescent City. Many hotels and brothels were also owned and operated by "mulatresses." And, of course, there were the "kept women"— the famous New Orleans quadroon *placées*, mistresses of Louisi-

1. This development, which routinely shocks and horrifies modern America, is not entirely surprising, for slavery was commonplace in West Africa when their ancestors were shipped as bondsmen to North America.

ana's white elite, and their children. These children—as well as the progeny of such unions in the rural parishes—were usually well provided for by their fathers. Before the Civil War such bequests were routinely formalized by fathers through acts of donation drawn up shortly before death or, more commonly, after the father had succumbed to familial pressure to take a white bride. On January 21, 1804, for example, shortly after his marriage to a white woman, Jacques Fontenette of St. Martinville gave Louise, his former mistress, and her nine mulatto children a parcel of land with five arpents frontage by forty arpents depth at Île à Labbé. The donation also included slaves. Other comparable donations included cash gifts.

The matriarchal households flourished, thanks to the business acumen of the remarkable women who sought to distance themselves and their children from the horrors of slavery as much and as quickly as possible. Among the most notable free black matriarchs were Marie Simien and Marie-Jeanne Lemelle of the Opelousas country. Simien, who settled at Opelousas with her four sons around 1796, wisely invested in real estate the money given to her by her former paramour. According to the 1818 tax rolls of St. Landry Parish, she owned 7,766 acres of farmland, 1,416 acres of which was considered prime real estate. Lemelle also quickly amassed a small fortune, thanks largely to 800 acres of land and fifteen slaves provided by her former common-law husband, François Lemelle, the son of a prominent white German Coast planter.

Such economically successful families modeled their existence upon that of the white Creole elite, whom they obsessively
emulated. This drive toward cultural amalgamation characterized not only the rural free blacks but also those of New Orleans. Like the white Creole elite, they became preoccupied
with status, and, because of the state's race-based, three-tiered
social system, skin color became a matter of growing importance among the free black elite. It is hardly surprising that
by 1860 virtually all free persons of color in rural southern
Louisiana were classified by census takers as mulattoes, a term
that, over the course of the nineteenth century, had come to
be increasingly suggestive of relatively light phenotypes.

Maintaining one's status was contingent upon economic and
familial stability. Antebellum travelers and modern historical
researchers agree that "on sugar estates, where the harvesting
and pressing of the cane demanded . . . sixteen- and eighteen-
hour workdays," free blacks "pushed their slaves incessantly." In
addition, like their white Creole counterparts, the *gens de
couleur libres* placed great emphasis on family cohesiveness and
stability. Second- and third-generation free black households
were consistently patriarchal in organization in the rural areas
and, in the late antebellum period, in New Orleans. This shift
in orientation reflects the pronounced tendency of free black
men to marry within their caste and to establish stable nuclear family units. The resulting network of blood ties and the
community's increasingly tenuous status under antebellum

Louisiana law helped to establish and reinforce a sense of identity within the caste.

Group cohesiveness was also strengthened by the community's almost universal respect for the tools necessary for success in a capitalist system—industriousness, frugality, diligence, and persistence. It is thus hardly surprising that, unlike many of their white counterparts in rural Louisiana, free people of color recognized the value of education. Many free black families sent boys to France for their schooling and professional training; many more were educated in private schools operated by free people of color in New Orleans and in the rural parishes. The black professionals who would emerge as leaders of the Reconstruction era were drawn from this group. These black professionals also constituted the city's African-American intelligentsia, operating pro-Republican, Reconstruction era newspapers and producing an important body of poetry and short stories.

Although the free black community blossomed intellectually in the postwar era, it was left in a quandary regarding the newly freed slaves. Like the white Creoles, the *gens de couleur libres* had come to view themselves as being innately superior to their neighbors. To differentiate themselves from the freedmen, the free blacks continued to identify themselves as *free people of color*—despite the fact that the term had lost all relevance—until the late 1890s in some southern Louisiana parishes. In the twilight years of the nineteenth century the former *gens de couleur libres* began to refer to themselves as Creoles—much to the horror of white Creoles, who began to insist that, like everything else in the kingdom of Jim Crow, admittance to their fraternity was limited to whites only.

The enduring gulf between white and black Creoles did little to foster a sense of racial unity between Creoles of Color and blacks. Although ambitious members of the free persons of color elite found it politically expedient to portray themselves as the spokesmen for freedmen after the Civil War, most former free persons of color would have nothing to do socially with the dark-hued former bondsmen. As the economic fortunes of the property-holding rural blacks fell as a result of wartime economic destruction, the former free blacks found that the distinction between themselves and the former slaves was gradually fading in the years after the war. As postbellum black codes destroyed the traditional intermediate caste, the mulattoes began to segregate themselves more and more from their black neighbors by means of their own private schools and such inventions as the "paper bag test" and the "comb test."[2] These social barriers were diminished, but not destroyed, during the

2. To pass the "paper bag test," persons seeking admission to a social function had to place a hand on a paper bag. Only persons whose phenotype was that shade or lighter were admitted. Persons passing the "comb test" had to have hair straight enough to permit passage of a comb's teeth.

Civil Rights movement, and tensions between these groups have persisted to the present, just as they have between white Creoles and Cajuns.

BLACK CREOLES

It is, therefore, most ironic that the most visible standard bearers of south Louisiana's ongoing Creole revival are descendants of freedmen, not free persons of color. Individuals who presently identify themselves as Creoles are generally descendants of French-speaking slaves who were emancipated during or immediately after the Civil War. Like the Creoles of Color, they are almost universally Catholic and largely French-speaking. These cultural characteristics set them apart from the English-speaking, Protestant majority within southern Louisiana's African-American community. Because the Francophone freedmen and their descendants demonstrated greater cultural affinity for the Creole of Color community, it is hardly surprising that, by 1910, the most economically successful members of this group began to intermarry with the least affluent Creoles of Color.

As in all modern societies, the poor and working classes have been the chief custodians of the vestiges of traditional culture. During the twentieth century members of the Creole of Color elite—like their counterparts in the white Creole and Cajun communities—did everything possible to move into the American mainstream as a means of availing themselves of the economic and social advantages that acceptance afforded. In the early twentieth century movement into the mainstream for the Creole of Color elite meant crossing the color line in the North, Midwest, or California. Those who could not cross the color line generally obtained college educations and moved into the ranks of the local professional and managerial classes in the wake of integration. By the late 1970s these migrations across class and cultural lines left the working class—dominated by the dark-complected descendants of Francophone freedmen (the black Creoles)—as heirs to the mantle of the Afro-Creole cultural tradition. This fact was tacitly recognized by the community in the following decade, as numerous individuals began to assume the Creole identity.

This development has had profound repercussions for the Creole cultural renaissance that began in the late 1980s. Unlike the descendants of the *gens de couleur libres,* who had generally maintained relatively cordial relations with white Francophones, the new black Creole leadership was openly antagonistic toward their white counterparts, who were in the midst of their own cultural revival. This animosity, resulting from decades of intense class and racial antagonism, was manifested in the organization of the Un-Cajun Committee and much inflammatory rhetoric by a small but highly vocal group of black Creole activists. In the late 1990s much of this rhetoric centered upon the Ragin' Cajun nickname of the University of Southwestern Louisiana's (now the University of Louisiana at Lafayette's) athletic teams, despite the fact that the school was established at the dawn of the twentieth century primarily to educate Cajun youth.

The anti-Cajun campaign stemmed in part from frustration among some Creole activists regarding the twenty-year head start that the Cajun cultural renaissance enjoyed. The Cajun cultural revival began as the local Civil Rights movement reached its peak, and, over the next two decades, as Cajun scholars began the work of defining the community for itself and the outside world, giving rise to ethnic pride, hundreds of locally owned businesses incorporated *Cajun* into their names. The Louisiana legislature recognized this grassroots movement by officially designating a twenty-two parish southern Louisiana region as Acadiana in 1971. Meanwhile, Creoles of Color, who at that time held a disproportionately large number of leadership positions in southern Louisiana Civil Rights organizations, continued to channel most of their energies into the cause of social and political equality until the late 1980s, when an embryonic Creole cultural revival began to take shape.

As with the Cajun cultural renaissance, the Creole revival was initially led by a coalition drawn from the elite and working classes, but grassroots activists quickly supplanted the social and cultural elite in shaping the course of the movement.

Limited interethnic cultural skirmishing resulted as that evolutionary track unfolded. Like all of the major ethnic revivals of the late twentieth century, the birth of the Creole renaissance was accompanied by an attempt to define group boundaries. Some activists undertook this task by defining what the group was *not*—hence, the Un-Cajun Committee.

The politics of exclusion had two major consequences. First, it diverted the community's attention from the process of defining itself for both Creoles and the outside world. It is indeed notable that in the 1980s and early 1990s all but one of the most significant studies of the Creole community were written or edited by whites. It is thus hardly surprising that the term *Creole* remains problematic in southern Louisiana, as is evidenced by the general lack of African-American businesses utilizing the term in their names. Second, the notoriety generated in the 1990s by inflammatory rhetoric obscured the common cultural base that Afro-Creoles share with their white cousins. As a result of nearly three centuries of interaction and cultural borrowing, both groups share a common language, religion, secular values, and, in recent years, culinary and musical repertoires. The parallels in their societal and cultural development are striking. But equally significant are the gulfs of prejudice and identity which separate these kindred communities. (Racial antipathy unfortunately is present on both sides of the rift.) It is tragically a case of "so close and yet so far."

CHAPTER FOUR

The Houma Nation

THE HOUMA NATION HAS ATTRACTED CONSID-
erable attention from Francophone linguists over the past
decade because French has been, and remains, the mother
tongue of most tribal members. Indeed, the authors of *The Historic Indian Tribes of Louisiana* maintain that "the Houma are
now the most conservative of all Louisiana French speakers"
(126). The sustained cultural interaction leading to the tribe's
linguistic transformation began in 1699, during Pierre Le
Moyne d'Iberville's ascent of the Mississippi River, an event
presaging the establishment of Louisiana's first permanent
French colony at Biloxi. On March 20 Iberville and his party arrived at the principal Houma village, located on the northern
edge of the large westward river's bend (the site of the present
Louisiana State Penitentiary at Angola). The Houma chief and

tribal elders welcomed the French explorers and held a feast in their honor.[1]

The following morning, Iberville, a Canadian well-versed in the importance of Indian diplomacy, participated in a calumet (peace pipe) ceremony effectively establishing an alliance between the Houma and the French. After departing the Houma village later that day, Iberville and his party returned to their ships anchored along the Gulf Coast. Before sailing for France, Iberville ordered construction of a fortification at present-day Ocean Springs, Mississippi, and assigned soldiers to the post, which maintained France's claim to the Mississippi Valley.

In 1700 Iberville solidified the embryonic Franco-Houma alliance by negotiating an end to a bitter territorial conflict between the Houma and the Bayougoula tribe, whose village was located on the site of the Iberville Parish hamlet presently bearing the latter tribe's name. The dispute centered upon alleged Bayougoula encroachments upon Houma hunting grounds. The boundary between Bayougoula and Houma hunting grounds was of course marked by the famous red pole—the "Iti Houma" (sometimes called Istrouma)—erected on a bluff in present-day

---

1. Iberville's account of the feast, the tribal costumes and customs, and the ritual dances performed in his honor provides perhaps the best ethnographic information regarding the Houma at the time of the initial European contacts.

Baton Rouge. Fighting between the two tribes had begun around June 1699, and by October the Houma had conducted at least two destructive raids on the Bayougoula village. During these raids the Houma captured large numbers of prisoners, whom they subsequently enslaved. The fortunes of this inter-tribal war changed abruptly in early 1700, when the Houma tribe, which had numbered six to seven hundred persons a year earlier, was decimated by "an abdominal flux"—probably dysentery or cholera. On March 4, 1700, Iberville, who had recently returned to Louisiana from France, intervened to prevent a major shift in the tribal balance of power. Iberville convened a meeting of the belligerent tribes' chiefs and negotiated a peace treaty.

The grateful Houma granted the French two important concessions. First, they allowed the French to assign a young boy to the village to learn the Houma language and serve as an official interpreter, and, second, they permitted a Catholic missionary to erect a fifty-foot-long chapel in the village square, opposite the tribal temple. Jesuit Father de Limoges took up residence in the village in late 1700, and the conversion of the Houma to Catholicism began shortly thereafter.

The closer relationship with the French which these developments entailed proved a double-edged sword for the Houma. On one hand, it provided them with a steady supply of French trade goods—particularly blankets, steel knives, muskets, and brandy—upon which the tribe became increasingly dependent; on the other hand, the Houma's economic dependence upon the French reduced the tribe to the status of a military client in the almost continual wars for imperial hegemony in North America. Beginning in 1704, the French utilized Houma to raid trans-Appalachian area tribes that had become trading partners with the British eastern seaboard colonies. The British responded in kind, and, in 1709 Jean-Baptiste Le Moyne de Bienville, Iberville's younger brother, reported that "the English of Carolina are sparing nothing to have our Indians destroyed by theirs."

As a result of intertribal hostilities between the French and British military proxies, the Houma were compelled to provide sanctuary to the Francophile Tunica tribe, which had been driven from its village by British-allied Alibamon and Chickasaw raiders. Around 1706 the Tunica then turned upon their hosts and, for unknown reasons, massacred more than half of the Houma tribe. The Houma survivors evidently fled initially to the banks of Bayou St. John in present-day New Orleans, but by 1709 they had migrated to a new village site near present-day Donaldsonville. In the following years the Houma appear to have maintained two village sites, one in modern Ascension Parish near present-day Burnside, on the east bank of the Mississippi River, and the other along Bayou Lafourche.

The remnants of the tribe gathered in the new villages constituted a pale reflection of the original Houma nation. By 1726 the tribe, which once reportedly boasted 175 to 400 warriors, could field only 50 men. Thirty years later its military strength still consisted of only 60 warriors, but the French doubted the potential effectiveness of these fighters because alcoholism had become rampant within the tribe.

Despite such terrible human toll paid for their alliance with the French, the Houma never wavered in their loyalty. The tribe routinely sent representatives to Mobile and, after 1718, to New Orleans to renew its alliance with the French, and in 1716 the Houma assisted the French by helping to negotiate a peace treaty with the Chitimacha tribe.

The diplomatic backdrop against which the Franco-Houma relationship existed changed radically in 1763. After suffering disastrous military reverses in the French and Indian War (1754–63), France partitioned Louisiana through the Treaty of Paris, ratified on February 10, 1763. The portion of Louisiana stretching from the Appalachian Mountains to the Mississippi River—with the exception of the Isle of Orleans (the area including New Orleans and bounded by the Mississippi River, Bayou Manchac, the Amite River, and lakes Maurepas and Pontchartrain)—was ceded to Great Britain. The portion of Louisiana west of the Mississippi and the Isle of Orleans were transferred to Spain.

As a result of the Treaty of Paris, the Houma faced not only the loss of their traditionally close partnership with the French colonial government but also encroachment by both their traditional British enemies and ostensibly friendly white settlers. Following the establishment of a British outpost at nearby Manchac, military authorities used Native American proxies— particularly the Talapousa tribe of the Creek confederacy—to harass and intimidate settlements in lower Spanish Louisiana. The Houma responded by first threatening violence against the British military for the caning of a French Louisianian by an English officer and later, in August 1765, by ransacking a British governmental warehouse at Manchac. Border tensions remained high throughout the early 1770s as a result of efforts of British Indian Agent John Thomas to persuade tribes along the intercolonial border to change allegiance.

The stress induced by border tensions was exacerbated by the encroachment of colonial settlers upon what the Houma had come to consider their tribal lands. In 1766 and 1767 Louisiana's Spanish colonial government began settling Acadian refugees along the Mississippi River, in present-day St. James, Ascension, and Iberville parishes. By the early 1770s Acadians and former German Coast settlers had begun to take up lands along upper Bayou Lafourche. The rapid Acadian population growth in the present Burnside and Donaldsonville areas quickly undermined relations between the exiles and their

Houma neighbors—relations that evidently had initially been harmonious.

Deteriorating relations resulted primarily from developments of the mid-1770s. In 1774 Houma chief Calabée sold the Burnside village site to Maurice Conway and Alexandre Latil. Seemingly unhappy with Calabée's leadership, the Houma then split into three bands. One group, consisting of twenty warriors and their families, remained on the Burnside village site and refused to leave, despite mounting pressure from the local and provincial governments. Another band migrated to vacant lands two and a half leagues upstream from the Burnside village, while a third group occupied the lands of established Acadian immigrants. Each of the Houma bands was governed by a chief, and the three chiefs were continuously at odds.

Preoccupation with the tribe's internal power struggle allowed an unnecessary confrontation to develop. Friction between the Acadians and the Houmas squatting on their lands escalated rapidly. In March 1778 Louis Judice, commandant of the Lafourche District, lamented "that the Houma Indians cause considerable harm to the settlers, stealing their rice and corn from the fields, rustling and killing their hogs which they subsequently sent to the English." Acting on the complaints of several aggrieved farmers, including Joseph Landry, who lost more than sixty barrels of corn to the Houma, Judice confronted the chief of the Houma band responsible for the thefts and warned that his village would be destroyed by the local militia if the raids did not cease.

Judice's warning went unheeded, but there was no military response. The Houma interpreted this as a sign of weakness, and the raiders became increasingly bold. By the early 1780s Houma tribal members raided Acadian farms by day, and, when their victims resisted, the Indians fired into their homes. Local authorities attributed the boldness of the Houma attackers to drunkenness resulting from illegal rum sales by local smuggler Jean Baptiste Chauvin.

An abortive slave insurrection in the Lafourche District in 1785 brought a temporary truce to the Acadian-Houma feud, for the local white population was obliged to hire the Houma to track down the slave fugitives hiding in the local swamps. Once the threat of a slave uprising had passed, however, Acadian-Houma relations again deteriorated.

Local interracial animosities simmered until May 1788, when a smallpox outbreak forced the Houma to abandon their villages and migrate down Bayou Lafourche to an undisclosed location. At this point the tribe as a collective entity disappears temporarily from the documentary record.

The gap in the documentation regarding the tribe has been a leading cause of the federal government's refusal to extend official recognition to the tribe. A few scattered references to tribal members suggest that a few Houma lived in the marginal backlands along either Bayou Lafourche or the Mississippi River in the Burnside area until around 1810. In addition, land records discovered by Houma researchers suggest that at least some of the tribe moved to lands granted to Louis Le Sauvage and two other Houmas in 1788. The tribe, however, had dispersed, and its members appear to have intermarried extensively with other Native American groups at this time, particularly with members of the Choctaw bands who had been given asylum by the Houma in the 1770s. Indeed, the few "Houma" remaining in the Burnside area at the dawn of the nineteenth century—only four families according to one source—reportedly spoke exclusively "Choctaw and French." The loss of native language was not confined to the Burnside band. The Houma vocabulary compiled in Terrebonne Parish by famous Native American Studies pioneer John R. Swanton in 1907 indicates that virtually all of the language was drawn from the Choctaw-based Mobilian trade dialect that was the lingua franca among the colonial-era French-allied tribes of the Southeast.

The loss of linguistic integrity was coupled with a loss of ascriptive identity. The remnants of the Houma tribe were so widely scattered at the end of the eighteenth century that, shortly after the Louisiana Purchase, American authorities began to report the group's extinction. The federal government supported the Territorial authorities' contention, maintaining that the tribe ceased to exist in the late eighteenth century, for the group had lost its traditional political organization. In addition, the federal government claimed that the scattered tribe had intermarried to such an extent that they could no longer be legitimately identified as Houma.

The apparent dissolution of the tribe, plus the absence of a written patent by the Spanish colonial government, caused the American Land Claims Commission to reject Houma claims to tribal lands in 1814. This decision stands in stark contrast to the action of the American Land Claims Commission in recognizing the land ownership of the Chitimacha, who had maintained their political integrity and identity in present-day St. Mary Parish.

The land commission, however, did honor the claims of individual Native Americans in Terrebonne Parish. The land claims of Louis Le Sauvage and two other Native Americans of unknown tribal affiliation served as the cradle of the modern Houma tribe. By 1830 the Native Americans who had gathered on these properties "had evolved into a 'single, geographical community.'" The undisputed leader of the community at this critical developmental period was Rosalie Courteaux, the niece of Louis Le Sauvage and the daughter of a Biloxi Indian. Rosalie Courteaux, who died in 1883, "was the last Houma leader reputed to have exercised any sort of broad authority over the general tribal membership."

Other Houma women, however, played equally important roles in the tribe's evolution through their capacity as cultural transmitters. Between 1830 and 1860 women in the new Houma community intermarried extensively with French-speaking men of the region, and it appears that the group's principal language became Cajun French as a result of exogamy during this period.

Around 1850 the Houma began migrating from the bayous of upper Terrebonne Parish to the coastal marshes to the south. The movement evidently stemmed in part from the group's increasing marginalization in local society. The 1850 census of Terrebonne Parish indicates that small Houma communities existed along Bayou Terrebonne, Bayou DuLarge, Bayou Petit Caillou, Bayou Pointe aux Chênes, Bayou Grand Caillou, and lower Bayou Lafourche. John R. Swanton found six Houma communities in the Lafourche-Terrebonne coastal marshes in 1907. In Terrebonne Parish the Houma tribal population grew slowly, from 103 in 1860 to 639 in 1920, 1,980 in 1960, and 3,274 in 1980.

Thrust into the coastal marsh region, the Houma were forced to adapt their survival skills to the harsh demands of their new environment. The tribal members learned to exploit local resources by developing new fishing techniques based upon the use of weirs.

But, as many aspects of their culture changed, the Houma

maintained their special status in local society. In 1907 Swanton reported that the "Houma 'form a distinct class of the [local] population, and prefer to be called Indians.'" This "Indian" classification, however, was clouded by the fact that a small portion of the tribe had intermarried with African Americans, giving rise to a tri-racial group known locally as "Sabines." The presence of the Sabine community confused the tribe's legal status in the era of Jim Crow (segregation).

In 1913 the Houma lost a court case seeking to force the Terrebonne Parish School Board to admit their children to white schools, the judge having ruled that the plaintiffs' children were "of the colored race" and, hence, could not attend white educational facilities. In June 1931 United States Department of the Interior investigator Roy Nash reported that "there is a five percent which shows unmistakable Negro blood, and that is where all the trouble lies. The whites will not admit any of the Indian mixed breeds to their school because of the possibility of admitting some one with a few drops of colored blood; the 'Indians' will not attend colored schools." Only in the 1950s was a state-sponsored Indian school built at Dulac, deep in the coastal marshes.

The construction of the school at Dulac provides tangible proof that Louisiana governmental agencies recognized the Houma's claim of Native American ancestry. The federal government concurs that this identity is indeed valid on the basis of external (ascriptive) classification by the local non-Indian population. But mere identification alone is insufficient basis for federal recognition. According to legal scholar Bruce Duthu, himself of Houma ancestry, "considerations of a persistent tribal community, descendancy from an historic tribe and sustained political authority or influence must also be" proved, "and on these points, according to the federal government, the Houmas' evidence falls short."

The lack of federal recognition has prevented the Houma tribe from opening and operating land-based casinos, and the poverty that has gripped the group for the past century persists. Educational levels and English proficiency remain low among the seventeen thousand individuals presently listed in the Houma Nation's tribal role. The 1990 census indicated that approximately 60 percent of the Houma residing in Terrebonne Parish and almost 50 percent of the Lafourche Parish Houma over five years of age spoke Cajun French as their first language. Approximately 20 percent of the Houma in both parishes reported that they did "not speak English very well."

The present status of the Houma in Louisiana is thus comparable to that of Cajuns of the late nineteenth century, when social isolation born of poverty served as the principal vehicle for cultural preservation. It will be interesting to see how long this unique culture endures as globalization extends its tentacles into the remote corners of this planet, including Louisiana's coastal marshes, and the nation's modern Louisiana homeland rapidly disappears in the face of coastal erosion and marsh-land subsidence, posing the threat that the Houma will be forced to migrate to inland communities.

French Louisiana Historiography

LOUISIANA HISTORIANS HAVE DISPLAYED ONLY sporadic interest in the state's French-speaking communities. During the antebellum era, when the field of Louisiana Studies was dominated by writers of French immigrant and white Creole ancestry, the standard histories of the Pelican State focused on the region's colonial and early national eras, when the Francophone population dominated both New Orleans and the densely settled plantation belt in the hinterlands. Scholarly interest in Louisiana's French experience flagged noticeably in the late nineteenth and early twentieth centuries, after a torrent of Anglo-American immigration reduced the state's once dominant Francophone population to minority status. Like other contemporary American minorities, Louisiana's French speakers were reviled in the popular media and ignored by the halls of academe.

The attention of scholars, formerly focused upon the state's once contentious Anglo-French struggle for political and cultural dominance, was redirected by deteriorating postbellum race relations to the Civil War and Reconstruction eras and the new regional social order they created. By the mid-twentieth century Louisiana's French-speaking communities were almost entirely forgotten in state histories and historical textbooks.

After the beginning of the Cajun cultural renaissance in 1968 and the national notoriety that Cajun music and cuisine attracted in subsequent decades, new generations of scholars—often of French descent—again turned their attention to the state's long-neglected French-speaking groups. The resulting research and publications have greatly expanded the public's depth and breadth of understanding regarding the Francophone experience in Louisiana, particularly the complexity of south Louisiana's intricate social, cultural, and linguistic mosaics.

PRIMARY SOURCES

MANUSCRIPTS

The explosion of late-twentieth-century scholarship was made possible in part by the efforts of various Louisiana repositories to build major archival collections documenting the origins and evolution of the state's various Francophone communi-

ties. Some of the leading documentary collections are located
at the Center for Louisiana Studies, the Acadian and Creole
Folklore and Folklife Archive, and the Southwestern Archives
of the University of Louisiana at Lafayette; the Historic New Orleans Collection; the T. Harry Williams Center for Oral History
and the Special Collections Division of Hill Memorial Library
at Louisiana State University in Baton Rouge; the Special Collections Division of Howard-Tilton Memorial Library at Tulane
University in New Orleans; and the ecclesiastical archives for
the Archdiocese of New Orleans and the dioceses of Lafayette,
Baton Rouge, Lake Charles, Houma-Thibodaux, and Alexan-
dria.[1]

Resources at these repositories generally consist of three
classes of materials: original manuscripts, microfilm copies
of manuscripts in European and Canadian repositories, and
recordings of interviews and musical performances. The documentary record easily eclipses its oral counterpart in terms
of bulk because literacy rates in Louisiana have traditionally
been low, and most of the extant documentation consists of
official administrative correspondence and memos.

Most of the major archival collections for early French
Louisiana are housed in the Archives des Colonies section of

1. Unlike the secular materials, religious records are generally difficult to
access because of use restrictions imposed by local prelates.

France's Archives Nationales, located in Paris. The Archives des Colonies is divided into fourteen archival series: A (*Actes de pouvoir souverain*), B (*Correspondance envoyée*), C (*Correspondance générale*), D (*Troupes des colonies*), E (*Personnel individuel*), F1A (*Fonds des colonies*), F2A (*Compagnies de commerce*), F2B (*Commerce aux colonies*), F2C (*Colonies en générale*), F3 (*Collection Moreau de Saint-Méry*), F4 (*Bureaux des contentieux*), F5A (*Missions religieuses*), F5B (*Passagers*), and G1 (*État civil*). Most of Louisiana's French colonial records are concentrated in series A, B, C, D, E, F3, and G1. Series A ostensibly consists of royal edicts, but the Louisiana materials—confined largely to volumes 22 and 23—are comprised of such diverse documents as the charter of Antoine Crozat's Company of Louisiana and documents regarding the establishment of the colony's quasi-legislative body and court of last resort, the Superior Council. The B series contains ministerial directives and royal appointments. Section 13a of the C series consists of the official correspondence of the colony's leading administrative officials. Series D includes muster rolls for the garrison at Louisiana's major settlements, while Series E contains dossiers for administrative and military personnel. The F3 series encompasses a variety of Louisiana materials in volumes 241–43, including transcripts of Superior Council sessions and documents pertaining to the arrival of Acadian refugees. Volumes 412, 464, and 465 of series G1 include most of the extant ship lists and census reports for early French Louisiana. Microfilm copies of the French colonial materials are available in several Louisiana repositories.

The French colonial manuscript collections provide the documentary building blocks for reconstructing the emergence of a Creole society in the Mississippi Valley. The administrative correspondence charts the introduction and development of social institutions, including the colony's three-tiered social system, which profoundly shaped the development of the black and white Creole communities. Bureaucratic reports also record the arrival of the first Acadians to reach Louisiana in the mid-1760s.

It is ironic that the richest source of information regarding the daily life of Louisiana's early Francophone communities is found not in French documentary collections but in Spanish period (1763–1803) documentary resources from Iberian repositories. The Spanish era documentary resources reside primarily in two manuscript collections at Seville's Archivo General de Indias—the Papeles Procedentes de Cuba and the Audiencia de Santo Domingo collection. The Louisiana materials in the Papeles Procedentes de Cuba, popularly known as the Cuba Papers,[2] are believed to consist of fifteen to seventeen million folios of records documenting virtually every phase of colo-

2. Spanish Louisiana was under the jurisdiction of the governor-general of Havana, Cuba.

nial life. The commandants' reports provide the best insight into the pioneers' mundane activities, Louisiana's emerging class system, the Acadian influx, and the adaptation of Old World immigrants (both African and European) to their New World circumstances and environment. The Audiencia de Santo Domingo papers, on the other hand, deal primarily with the workings of the upper echelons of the colonial government, but the collection does contain important documentation regarding the 1785 Acadian migration from France to Louisiana as well as dossiers documenting the Spanish military careers of white Creoles.

The embarrassment of documentary riches dating from the Spanish period contrasts with the relative paucity of documentation for the Territorial (1803–11) and Antebellum (1812–60) eras. The Historic New Orleans Collection, the Louisiana and Lower Mississippi Valley Collections in Hill Memorial Library at Louisiana State University–Baton Rouge, and Southwestern Archives at the University of Louisiana at Lafayette house many of the most historically significant early-nineteenth-century documentary collections. The small number of extant letters, diaries, and memoirs is partially offset by the ready availability of huge caches of "nontraditional" resources. Invaluable historical information can also be found in French-language and bilingual newspapers, port records and ship lists, federal census reports, civil records in parish courthouses, and published travelogues. The travelogues are particularly noteworthy because of their pivotal role in shaping the ascriptive stereotypes that presently frame the manner in which Louisiana's Francophone communities are viewed by the outside world.

Traditional documentary resources are equally scarce in twentieth-century archival collections, but researchers can glean demographic data from available federal census reports, particularly the 1910 decennial census report, which indicates the linguistic orientation of each enumerated individual. Governmental data are complemented by the recordings in Louisiana's premier oral history and folklore collections. The world's largest collection of Acadian and Creole oral history, folklore, and folklife recordings is stored in the Center for Acadian and Creole Folklore, housed in the Center for Cultural and Eco-Tourism at the University of Louisiana at Lafayette.

PRIMARY SOURCES

PUBLICATIONS

Investigators utilizing primary source documentation face a variety of challenges, ranging from limits on accessibility imposed by privacy laws to language barriers. Louisiana's amateur historical researchers have traditionally found the issue of language to be particularly problematic, for, although they are often bilingual, they are not usually literate in French, the language in which most of the relevant colonial era documents are written, even in the Spanish period. Colonialists, however, published only a limited number of translated and annotated documentary compilations. For the French period monolingual researchers should consult the following representative works: Carl A. Brasseaux, trans. and ed., *A Comparative View of French Louisiana: The Journals of Pierre Le Moyne d'Iberville and Jean-Jacques-Blaise d'Abbadie, 1699 and 1762* (Lafayette, La., 1979); and Dunbar Rowland and A. G. Sanders, trans. and eds., *Mississippi Provincial Archives: The French Dominion*, rev. and ed. Patricia K. Galloway, 5 vols. (Jackson, Miss., and Baton Rouge, La., 1927–84). Researchers seeking translations of Acadian materials should refer to Carl A. Brasseaux, trans., ed., and annot., *Quest for the Promised Land: Official Correspondence Relating to the First Acadian Migration to Louisiana, 1764–1769* (Lafayette, La., 1989); and George Reinecke, trans. and ed., "Early Louisiana French Life and Folklore: From the Anonymous Breaux Manuscript, as Edited by Professor Jay K. Ditchy," *Louisiana Folklore Miscellany* 2 (1966): 1–58. Prefect Pierre Clément de Laussat's *Memoirs of My Life to My Son during the Years 1803 and After, Which I Spent in Public Service in Louisiana as Commissioner of the French Government for the Retrocession to France of That Colony and for Its Transfer to the United States* (Baton Rouge, 1978) provides an excellent description of early white Creole life in the lower Mississippi Valley.

SECONDARY SOURCES

BIBLIOGRAPHIES

Firsthand accounts of life and events provide the raw materials for scholarly studies of Louisiana's Francophone experience in recent years. Despite the flurry of publishing activity in the area of Francophone Studies, few guides to the secondary literature exist. Carl A. Brasseaux and Glenn R. Conrad, *A Bibliography of Scholarly Literature on Colonial Louisiana and New France* (Lafayette, La., 1992), is the most comprehensive available bibliography on Louisiana's colonial experience. For good but dated guides to the literature on Louisiana's Acadian community, see Pearl Mary Segura, *The Acadians in Fact and Fiction: A Classified Bibliography of Writing on the Subject of Acadians in Stephens Memorial Library, Southwestern Louisiana Institute, Lafayette, Louisiana* (Baton Rouge, 1955); and Carl A. Brasseaux and Michael James Forêt, *A Selected Bibliography of Acadian History, Culture, and Genealogy, 1955–1985* (Thibodaux, La., 1985). There are, unfortunately, no comparable bibliographies for Creole Studies.

BOOKS AND ARTICLES

The sections that follow provide a cursory guide to the leading publications on the major population groups discussed in the essays in this book. This selected bibliography is designed to provide newcomers to the field with an initial roadmap to the literature.

French Colonial Louisiana

The best concise account of the founding and early development of Louisiana (1699–1732) is Mathé Allain, "Not Worth a Straw": French Colonial Policy and the Early Years of Louisiana (Lafayette, La., 1988). The most comprehensive treatment of Louisiana's early years can be found in Marcel Giraud, History of French Louisiana, trans. Brian Pearce, 5 vols. (Baton Rouge, 1974–87). There is no thorough study of Louisiana during the 1730s, but Guy Frégault's Le Grand Marquis: Pierre de Rigaud de Vaudreuil et la Louisiane (Montreal, 1952) provides a political history of the colony for the 1740s and early 1750s. Marc de Villiers du Terrage, The Last Years of French Louisiana, trans. Hosea Phillips, ed. Carl A. Brasseaux and Glenn R. Conrad (Lafayette, La., 1982), provides the best account of the tumultuous final years of French colonial rule in the Mississippi Valley.

Acadians/Cajuns

The closing years of French rule and the beginning of the Spanish era witnessed the Acadian migration to the lower Mississippi Valley. The Acadian diaspora, once a lost chapter in North American history, has become in recent years one of the most closely scrutinized episodes in eighteenth-century American history because of its resemblance to the tragic ethnic cleansing exercises of the 1990s. Persons seeking information regarding the pre-dispersal experiences of the Acadians should consult Andrew Hill Clark, *Acadia: The Geography of Early Nova Scotia to 1760* (Madison, Wis., 1968); and Naomi E. S. Griffiths, *The Acadians: Creation of a People* (Toronto, 1973). On circumstances producing the Acadian deportation, see Naomi E. S. Griffiths, *The Acadian Deportation: Deliberate Perfidy or Cruel Necessity?* (Toronto, 1969); and Geoffrey Plank, *An Unsettled Conquest: The British Campaign against the Peoples of Acadia* (Philadelphia, 2001).

The post-dispersal Acadian wanderings are covered in Carl A. Brasseaux, *Scattered to the Wind: Dispersal and Wanderings of the Acadians, 1755–1809* (Lafayette, La., 1991). The Acadian migration to Louisiana is detailed in Brasseaux, *The Founding of New Acadia: Beginnings of Acadian Life in Louisiana, 1765–1803* (Baton Rouge, 1987). And Brasseaux, *Acadian to Cajun: Transformation of a People, 1803–1877* (Jackson, Miss., 1992), analyzes the transformation of Acadian society as it adapted to new circumstances in Acadiana. There is no comprehensive study of Acadian society between the end of Reconstruction (1877) and the American entry into World War II (1941). Lauren C. Post, *Cajun Sketches from the Prairies of Southwest Louisiana* (Baton Rouge, 1962), remains the best study of Cajun life in the early-to mid-twentieth century. For an account of the Cajun experience during the 1927 flood, when 100,000 persons were displaced in Acadiana, see Carl A. Brasseaux and Glenn R. Conrad, *Crevasse! The 1927 Flood in Acadiana* (Lafayette, La., 1994). Two recently published works trace the accelerating pace of cultural change within the Cajun community in the late twentieth century: Shane K. Bernard, *The Cajuns: Americanization of a People* (Jackson, Miss., 2003); and Jacques M. Henry and Carl L. Bankston III, *Blue Collar Bayou: Louisiana Cajuns in the New Economy of Ethnicity* (Westport, Conn., 2002).

Creoles

Over the course of their long history in Louisiana, Acadians have interacted most frequently with their Creole neighbors. Members of Louisiana's Creole community span the full range of the racial spectrum, but in the late nineteenth and early twentieth centuries the New Orleans social elite mounted a concerted effort to ensure that all published references to Creoles referred exclusively to whites. Thus, it is hardly surprising that early Creole historiography was rigidly circumscribed by this entirely artificial boundary, and popular and scholarly studies of Louisiana Creoles focused exclusively upon the wealthiest members of the white Creole community in the Crescent City and southern Louisiana plantation belt for decades.

That focus began to change in midcentury, when Joseph Tregle Jr., scion of a Creole family, began publishing the most authoritative works on the white Creole community, studies that effectively challenged the prevailing beliefs that Creoles were exclusively white, wealthy, and inherently superior to their neighbors. Tregle's groundbreaking essay "Early New Orleans Society: A Reappraisal," *Journal of Southern History* 18 (1952): 21–36, remains the most influential of his writings. In addition, Joseph Tregle's essay "Creoles and Americans," in Arnold R. Hirsch and Joseph Logsdon, eds., *Creole New Orleans: Race and Americanization* (Baton Rouge, La., 1992), 131–88, provides the best account of the late-nineteenth-century decline of the Crescent City's white Creole community. For a nostalgic view of the urban Creole community's twilight years, see Leonard V. Huber, *Creole Collage: Reflections on the Colorful Customs of Latter-Day New Orleans Creoles* (Lafayette, La., 1980).

Huber, citing a prominent white New Orleanian, identifies Creoles as "native Louisianians of French or Spanish ancestry, or both." Tregle discredits the validity of this narrow definition of the term in an article entitled "On That Word 'Creole' Again: A Note," *Louisiana History* 23 (1982): 193–98.

Indeed, throughout the colonial period, the term *Creole* was also applied to the offspring of African immigrants. James H. Dormon's *Creoles of Color of the Gulf South* (Knoxville, Tenn., 1996) provides the best introduction to Louisiana's Afro-Creole experience. Gwendolyn Midlo Hall's *Africans in Colonial Louisi-*

ana: The Development of Afro-Creole Culture in the Eighteenth Century (Baton Rouge, 1992) defines the historical backdrop against which the Creole of Color community developed. Gary Mills's highly regarded study *The Forgotten People: Cane River's Creoles of Color* (Baton Rouge, 1977), a work focusing on the Isle Breville / Cane River community of northwestern Louisiana, set the standard by which all subsequent scholarly work on the Creoles of Color has been judged. *Creoles of Color in the Bayou Country,* by Carl A. Brasseaux, Keith P. Fontenot, and Claude F. Oubre (Jackson, Miss., 1994), examines the origins and evolution of Louisiana's largest rural Creole communities, located in the area bounded by Bayou Teche and the Texas border. Two more recent works of interest include Hirsch and Logsdon, *Creole New Orleans: Race and Americanization;* and Sybil Kein, ed., *Creole: The History and Legacy of Louisiana's Free People of Color* (Baton Rouge, La., 2000). The Kein anthology consists of an eclectic collection of essays examining the issues of Creole identity, race relations across Louisiana's three-tiered (white, mulatto, and black) racial society, and the African origins of Creole cuisine and language. Other, more narrowly focused works on the Creole of Color community include Virginia R. Dominguez, *White by Definition: Social Classification in Creole Louisiana* (New Brunswick, N.J., 1986); and Caryn Cossé Bell, *Revolution, Romanticism, and the Afro-Creole Protest Tradition in Louisiana, 1718–1868* (Baton Rouge, La, 1997).

Architecture

Architecture is perhaps the most thoroughly studied facet of Creole and Cajun culture. For the best introduction to Louisiana's indigenous architectural forms, see Jonathan Fricker, Donna Fricker, and Patricia L. Duncan, *Louisiana Architecture: A Handbook on Styles* (Lafayette, La., 1998). For an excellent, encapsulated description of Acadian folk architecture, see R. Warren Robison, "Louisiana Acadian Domestic Architecture," in Steven L. Del Sesto and Jon L. Gibson, eds., *The Culture of Acadiana: Tradition and Change in South Louisiana* (Lafayette, La., 1975), 63–78. Jay D. Edwards, *Louisiana's Remarkable Vernacular Architecture, 1700–1900* (Baton Rouge, La., 1988), is the best source of information about ancillary structures on Cajun and Creole farmsteads. On the origins of Louisiana's Cajun and Creole architectural styles, see Samuel Wilson Jr., *The Architecture of Colonial Louisiana: Collected Essays of Samuel Wilson, Jr.*, ed. Jean M. Farnsworth and Ann M. Masson (Lafayette, La., 1987); and Fred Daspit, *Louisiana Architecture, 1714–1830* (Lafayette, La., 1996). Persons interested in urban Creole architecture should consult the fine New Orleans Architecture series, published by Pelican Press of Gretna, Louisiana.

Language, Folklore, and Folklife

Linguists and folklorists, unlike historians, have consistently maintained intense interest in French Louisiana. For an introduction to Cajun and Creole French, see Hosea Phillips, "The Spoken French of Louisiana," in Glenn R. Conrad, ed., *The Cajuns: Essays on Their History and Culture* (Lafayette, La., 1978), 173–84. For a more exhaustive study of the subject, see Albert V. Valdman, ed., *French and Creole in Louisiana* (New York, 1997).

For the most comprehensive introduction to Cajun and Creole folklore, see Barry Jean Ancelet, *Cajun and Creole Folktales: The French Oral Tradition of South Louisiana* (Jackson, Miss., 1994). See also the introduction to Carl Lindahl, Maida Owens, and C. Renée Harvison, eds., *Swapping Stories: Folktales from Louisiana* (Jackson and Baton Rouge, 1997). The Evangeline story remains a centerpiece of southern Louisiana lore. Carl A. Brasseaux, *In Search of Evangeline: Birth and Evolution of the Evangeline Myth* (Thibodaux, La., 1988), traces the story's origins and development while also analyzing its claims in light of the documentary record. For an introduction to the folklore of the Houma tribe, see Bruce Duthu, "Folklore of the Louisiana Houma Indians," *Louisiana Folklife* 4 (1979): 1–33.

For an excellent overview of Cajun and Creole folklife, see Nicholas R. Spitzer, *Louisiana Folklife: A Guide to the State* (Baton Rouge, 1985). See Barry Jean Ancelet et al., *Cajun Country,* Folklife in the South Series (Jackson, Miss., 1991), for the best study of Cajun folklife. See also Allen Begnaud and Jon L. Gibson, "Cajun Folk Occupations: A Summary," in Steven L. Del Sesto and Jon L. Gibson, eds., *The Culture of Acadiana: Tradition and*

Change in South Louisiana (Lafayette, La., 1975), 50–62. Malcolm L. Comeaux, *Atchafalaya Swamp Life: Settlement and Folk Occupations* (Baton Rouge, La., 1972), remains the best study of Cajun folklife in the remote Atchafalaya Basin.

Mardi Gras

Mardi Gras is perhaps the French cultural institution most widely associated with Louisiana by the outside world. There are two quite different varieties—an urban celebration that glorifies social hierarchies and the rural carnival that turns the existing social order on its head. For information on Acadiana's distinctive *Courir de Mardi Gras*, see Barry Jean Ancelet, *"Capitaine, voyage ton flag": The Traditional Cajun Country Mardi Gras* (Lafayette, La., 1989). On the urban celebration, see Sam Kinser, *Carnival, American Style: Mardi Gras at New Orleans and Mobile* (Chicago, 1990).

Cajun and Creole Cuisine

The popularity of Cajun and Creole cuisine made cookbooks and "cookbook histories" a major cottage industry in late-twentieth-century southern Louisiana. Unfortunately, much of the information contained in these publications is speculative at best, and solid, comprehensive studies of the development of Cajun and Creole cuisine remain to be written. For a light overview of the similarities and differences between Cajun and

Creole cooking, see Ernest Gueymard, "Louisiana's Creole-Acadian Cuisine," *Louisiana Review* 2 (1973): 8–19. Literary luminary Lafcadio Hearn provides the best description of early Creole cuisine in the *Creole Cook Book: A Literary and Culinary Adventure* (1885; rpt., New Orleans, 1967). C. Paige Gutierrez, *Cajun Foodways* (Jackson, Miss., 1992), provides the best introduction to Cajun cuisine. Colette Guidry Leistner, "French and Acadian Influences upon the Cajun Cuisine of Southwest Louisiana" (M.A. thesis, University of Southwestern Louisiana, 1986), provides greater detail about the evolutionary path taken by Cajun cooking over the past two centuries.

Cajun Music and Zydeco

In recent years Cajun music and zydeco, both products of extended interaction between the Cajun and Creole of Color communities, have drawn considerable popular and scholarly interest. Barry Jean Ancelet, *Cajun Music: Its Origins and Development* (Lafayette, La., 1989), provides an excellent overview of the genre and its intimate relationship with zydeco. A much more detailed look at the genre's early development can be found in Ann Allen Savoy, *Cajun Music: A Reflection of a People* (Eunice, La., 1986). Barry Ancelet, *The Makers of Cajun Music: Musiciens cadiens et créoles* (Austin, Tex., 1984), provides a behind-the-scenes look at the musicians who helped shape and perpetuate the sounds that took the nation by storm in the late twentieth century. Readers interested in Creole music should consult Ben Sandmel, *Zydeco!* (Jackson, Miss., 1999); and Nicholas Spitzer, "Zydeco and Mardi Gras: Creole Identity and Performance Genres in Rural French Louisiana" (Ph. D. diss., University of Texas, 1986); and Michael Tisserand, *The Kingdom of Zydeco* (New York, 1998).

Cajun and Creole musicians who came of age in the 1950s and early 1960s created a new, heavily Americanized sound popularly called "Swamp Pop." For the best account of this genre, see Shane K. Bernard, *Swamp Pop: Cajun and Creole Rhythm and Blues* (Jackson, Miss., 1996). John Broven, *South to Louisiana: The Music of the Cajun Bayous* (Gretna, La., 1983), discusses Swamp Pop as well as more traditional regional musical varieties.

Foreign French

Despite their large numbers, the nineteenth-century "Foreign French" immigrants have attracted remarkably little attention among Louisiana historians. For information regarding the Bonapartist refugees, see Simone Rivière de La Souchère Deléry, *Napoleon's Soldiers in America* (Gretna, La., 1972). On the French immigrants who disembarked at the port of New Orleans between 1820 and 1852, refer to Carl A. Brasseaux, *The "Foreign French": Nineteenth-Century French Immigration into Louisiana*, 3 vols. (Lafayette, La., 1990–93).

Houmas

The Houma nation has been chronically ignored by Louisiana Studies scholars, in part because of the group's physical isolation and in part because of linguistic barriers. For background information about the tribe, readers should consult Frederick Webb Hodge, *Handbook of American Indians, North of Mexico,* Smithsonian Institution Bureau of American Ethnology Bulletin 30, 2 vols. (Washington, D.C., 1912); John R. Swanton, *Indian Tribes of the Lower Mississippi Valley and Adjacent Coast of the Gulf of Mexico* (New York, 1911); John R. Swanton, *The Indians of the Southeastern United States,* Smithsonian Institution Bureau of American Ethnology Bulletin 137 (Washington, D.C., 1946); and Fred B. Kniffen et al., *The Historic Indian Tribes of Louisiana: From 1542 to the Present* (Baton Rouge, 1987). The best tribal history to date is Greg Bowman and Janel Curry-Roper, *The Houma People of Louisiana: A Story of Indian Survival* (Houma, La., 1982). In "The Houma Indians of Louisiana: The Intersection of Law and History in the Federal Acknowledgment Process," *Louisiana History* 38 (1997): 409–36, Bruce Duthu examines the struggle of the Houma people to achieve recognition by the Bureau of Indian Affairs.

CONCLUSION

Although much has been done in recent years, much remains to be done. Remarks interspersed throughout this narrative point to some of the major gaps in the existing literature, and some topics that have been studied should be revisited. For example, the role of religion in the Cajun and Creole communities—too long the province of the Catholic clergy or church employees—requires objective reevaluation, and the migration of thousands of Cajuns and Creoles into Protestant evangelical and Christian fundamentalist sects awaits scholarly examination and analysis. Musical historians and ethnomusicologists must finally view Cajun and Creole music globally, looking beyond the overly narrow confines of "traditional" music. In addition, the time has come for a comprehensive review of race relations in French-speaking Louisiana; this topic is particularly important because the modern Cajun and Creole communities are both products of cross-cultural borrowing across a local racial divide. An equally great cultural gulf separates rural members of the Cajun, Creole, and Houma communities from their urban cousins, yet these differences have yet to be studied.

Scholars have yet to explore the complex relationship between humans and their environment in Acadiana, a subject of tremendous relevance as the area's vulnerable wetlands are literally washed away, threatening the continued existence of regional subcultures that exist in these remote and forbidding habitats. Environmental factors also profoundly shaped the local societies' material culture, yet another subject that awaits comprehensive analysis.

Finally, comprehensive studies of the Acadians, Creoles, and Houmas are desperately needed. James H. Dormon's excellent overview of the Acadian/Cajun experience—*The People Called Cajuns: Introduction to an Ethnohistory* (Lafayette, La., 1983)—is dated, and there is nothing comparable for the Creole and Houma communities, despite the upsurge in publications on these groups in recent years. Not until these gaps in the literature are filled will insiders and outsiders alike begin to understand the world of Louisiana's Francophones.

Index